W9-BLL-699

COLIN DAVIS

Alan Blyth

Drake Publishers Inc
NEW YORK

ISBN 0–87749–365–0
Library of Congress Catalog Card No. 72–6428

Published in 1973 by Drake Publishers Inc
381 Park Avenue South, New York, N.Y. 10016

Printed in Great Britain

❧ *Contents* ❧

✤Introduction✤

Colin Davis—aged 30.

On Sunday October 18, 1959 Colin Davis was "born" as a conductor. Or so it seemed to a great number of people who, up to then, had hardly heard of him. That was the night he took over a concert performance of *Don Giovanni* from Klemperer at short notice and apparently made such a success of it that he was soon being claimed as Beecham's natural heir. That evening he took only a couple of bows after the performance before leaving the ecstatic applause to the distinguished cast (including Sutherland and Schwarzkopf). Perhaps he already sensed, as he certainly did not long after, that he was not fitted yet for the kind of acclaim that was being given him. In England we love to suddenly "discover" someone in the arts without ever regarding the consequences of such instant fame to the person concerned.

Colin Davis was then 32, and perhaps he should have been old enough to cope with the new situation, but as he puts it himself: "I wasn't ready to be the kind of success that I was supposed to be." He didn't feel prepared to take off on the international magic carpet that was being laid out for him. He felt he had made a good job of that *Don Giovanni*, but then he had known *Don Giovanni* for many years and he had not assumed, as some supposed, special powers, nor could he, as he has said, become part of the "fantasy life of other people".

Besides, until this occasion, nothing had happened to set him apart from his colleagues, although many who knew him well, or had worked with him, believed that he was the outstanding British conductor of his generation, certainly of Berlioz and Mozart, and probably of Stravinsky too. Since that time, of course, everything he has done has been watched with the keenest public and critical interest, so that maybe the years of trial and error spent in comparative obscurity have paid off.

He was born at Weybridge in Surrey on September 25, 1927, the third of three brothers in a family of seven. His mother played the piano slightly in the way of late Victorian mothers and his father had a pleasing light tenor. Apparently, when he was a very little boy Colin listened to records with considerable attention. His father had a large collection, including a great deal of Elgar, Delius, Sibelius, Debussy and "great chunks of Wagner" (all that was available then), and when as a boy he heard Melchior in *Siegfried*, it seemed to him like some terrible rite. It was a central topic of conversation in the family—the taste of music, rather than any technical discussion.

He did not learn the piano, which was something of a disadvantage later in his career, but he says there is no good regretting that now. Besides, he believes that the instrument has obvious drawbacks; it does not breathe and you cannot do anything expressive with it except play it loud or soft. The sensuousness of a violin or voice, he feels, are simply not there.

At this time, music was a very private thing for Colin. He longed to be alone, not to go for a walk with mother but to sit down and play the third act of *Siegfried*. He already had an absolute passion for music and used to play his father's collection over and over again.

Two of his older sisters, Audrey and Yvonne, have fairly vivid memories of Colin as a small boy. He liked animals, collected butterflies, enjoyed games, particularly cricket. Yvonne was at the same primary school during this period and they both nicknamed it the "tin school" because most of the rooms consisted of corrugated-iron huts. There were apparently quite a few tough boys at the school, who became Colin's friends, and were not received exactly with open arms in the Davis household. Yvonne, so Colin told her many years later, annoyed him very much by never waiting to go to school with him and at that time they were very definitely not good friends. Indeed, it seems that Colin's position in the family, a boy between pairs of girls, affected him considerably. He was frequently called on to fetch and carry for them, and this undoubtedly made him unhappy at times.

At the age of about nine, he began to become more of a loner, reading a great deal, and it was then that he started listening to records. Already when much smaller he could apparently decide what was on a disc even before he could read the label. Howard, the elder of his two brothers, who was killed in the war, helped him and encouraged him in his music, and his parents were not unsympathetic.

Later when he was at boarding school, he became very intense and passionate; he used to come home and, as Yvonne says, preach to them. "He thought we were half-baked, probably because we didn't appreciate his music enough. We tried to tell him that there *were* other things besides music. Not that we were against his interest in it; in fact we always gave him miniature scores for his birthday."

Today he is on good terms with all his sisters, and one of the younger ones, Heather, was his secretary for several years. She recalls, too, how kind Colin was to her when she was a little girl, paying for her to have piano lessons and always taking her to concerts.

As a small boy.

Family dissensions and some financial hardship during Colin's adolescence cannot have helped his presence of mind, and it was probably as well that he went to boarding school for much of it. He went in for a scholarship at King's School, Wimbledon, where the family was now living. He failed, largely, as his mother felt because he was nervous. She understood him well and backed him up all along. Having persuaded the authorities to let him sit the exam again, she was delighted when he passed. However, by now one of his brothers was finishing at Christ's Hospital, and so a vacancy existed for Colin to go there.

He was the last of three brothers to go to the school. The others knew a good deal about music but they had not done anything actively about it. Colin went to Christ's Hospital in 1938.

❧ Schooling ❧

So in 1938 he went to Christ's Hospital. There he was encouraged by his house-captain John Stevens to take up an instrument. He chose the clarinet, which he was soon playing in the school band. Then, as he puts it: "When I became adolescent, music took over." However, most people at school tried to persuade him not to be a musician; instead he was to be a doctor, because he was rather good at biology and chemistry. He took no notice of those who told him that it was a deplorable life as a musician, knowing that this was the only thing he wanted to do. He believes that an aspiring musician should be tested in this way as a sort of weeding out process. However, he does regret that he did not do more actual learning at school because of his passion for music, listening to records, learning the clarinet, and playing chamber music with friends. He also tried various other instruments, including the bassoon, to see how they worked. The school band met two or three times a week and played marches, Bizet's *L'Arlésienne*, selections from musicals, the overture to *Don Giovanni*. Several of the masters also encouraged Colin, playing sonatas with him, the Beethoven Septet, and so on. He feels that he needed this sort of encouragement and he responded to it.

Music offered him at this time some kind of independent strength, a hiving-off from the rest of the world. That is a feeling that has persisted. "It's like a Tarnhelm, or some kind of magic shield, which wards off the slings and arrows. It's a world into which you can slip. You might call it a psychosis. I look at it, however, as a kind of alchemy that transforms reality into an imaginative possibility. That's what Mozart really achieves."

Colin had already decided secretly on music as a career when at 14 he went to a performance of Beethoven's Seventh Symphony at Kingston. Doors were suddenly opened to him and he became totally involved in the art. He found in this work a directness, a tremendous sense of enjoyment, and it carried him on to all the Viennese classics. This utter absorption in music could not be shaken by anything or anyone.

Meanwhile he was forsaking records for scores, which he began to devour voraciously. He already had another secret desire—to be a conductor. At school he was once allowed to conduct the band but he remembers little about the occasion except that it was not much of a success. He used to conduct to his scores. His masters still remained unconvinced about music as a career, one going as far as to say depressingly and sar-

In a school group portrait at Christ's Hospital.

Above: In the Household Cavalry

Right: Portrait taken during days at the Royal College of Music.

castically that he would come and "hold the hat for you." Undeterred, Colin won a scholarship for the clarinet to the Royal College of Music, where he studied with Frederick Thurston. Technically far below many of his co-students, he began to work very hard to catch up. He felt that many of the people who *did* play very well looked down on him for his lack of technique and, in a sense, disliked his love of music.

This is born out by fellow-students of the time who suggest that the music above all was in Colin's mind. While they were concerned to get on with their own instrument, plough their own furrow, he was concerned with the whole musical picture. He was also withdrawn and somewhat introspective. As a clarinet player, he was to a certain extent overshadowed by Gervase de Peyer, who was probably the star among all the wood-winds during Colin's period at the College. After various attempts, he was forbidden to conduct and he could not get into the conducting class because he did not play the piano. Indeed, he began to fear that his inability in this respect might keep him forever from conducting.

Inside he felt he had something to express. In the meantime the army beckoned and he joined the Household Cavalry as a bandsman. Rejected as officer material, he continued, as he puts it "to hold the lowest rank— as musician and trooper." It was a fairly easy life. The band had to play at parades and suppers for George VI. Colin did not find it entirely an idle time, managing to practise a great deal. Stationed at Windsor, he was strategically placed to attend almost as many concerts as he liked in London at the Albert Hall, and he heard conductors like Beecham, Bruno Walter and Eduard van Beinum.

He now felt that he must try to organise an outlet for his desire to conduct. Gradually a group of players at the College who were interested in more than just their own instruments came together, first to play chamber music, then to tackle symphonies. When they moved to orchestral music, they formed themselves into the Kalmar Orchestra and, looking round for a conductor, they naturally turned to Colin. They met on Wednesdays in the echoing basement of the Ethical Church, Bayswater. Colin and others recall that their meetings were a cross between concerts, rehearsals and parties. Basically they were playthroughs of pieces they all wanted to get to know.

Most of the players, who have now gone on to be our leading chamber-music instrumentalists, appreciated Colin's dedication and enthusiasm. Mozart was, and is, his greatest love. Out of Kalmar came the Chelsea Opera Group, which began by giving performances of Mozart's operas at Oxford and Cambridge that still linger in the memory of those that heard them. The C.O.G. was started by Stephen Gray and David Cairns. Gray chose Colin on the strength of a recommendation of Gray's sister who praised his Mozart. Cairns first met Davis at Crosby Hall in 1949 when he was conducting *The Impresario* and playing in one of Mozart's wind serenades. Apart from *The Impresario*, his *Don Giovanni* in February 1950 with the Chelsea Opera Group was his first appearance as a conductor. He went up to the house of Cairns's parents the night before the performance, and he and the cast ran through the score.

Nobody concerned with the performance had met anybody quite like Colin before. His confidence in himself and his directness, his lack of inhibition, struck them immediately. I can recall that the same quality came across to those lucky enough to be in the audience. Robert Ponsonby, who is now administrator of the Scottish National Orchestra, and was singing Masetto, came up to Cairns at rehearsal and said incredulously "Colin's wonderful". People apparently said at that time that Colin was conceited and rude, but none of these things struck those taking part. All the young musicians of the time, who had a consuming passion for Mozart, were only too willing to play under him, because here was someone who understood Mozart. Egon Wellesz, then professor in Oxford, and Leonie Gombrich, who had known Busch's Mozart and other German interpreters, felt that Colin was a sort of reincarnation of Mozart—the spirit had descended on Colin, so they said.

The audience overflowed into the entrance to Holywell Music Room. At the beginning of the second act Colin stopped the orchestra after the first string chords and said "Come on strings, you can do better than that". This astounded the audience, who had not met anything like it before.

Meanwhile Colin, who was taking what engagements came his way as a clarinettist, played sufficiently often in orchestras to discover how difficult it was. Among others, he played second clarinet with Alec Sherman's New London Orchestra and at Glyndebourne under Fritz Busch in *Così fan tutte*. However, once you become known as a conductor, you are immediately struck off the list that orchestras keep of roving, free-lance instrumentalists. So it was with Colin when he took a job with what remained of the Ballet Russe. After three months, the whole venture collapsed leaving Colin stranded. By this time he had married the soprano April Cantelo and they had had a daughter, so that they were bound to worry about where Colin's next engagement was to come from, although his wife was already running a successful career.

Bernard Robinson's Music Camp helped him to keep up his spirits; so did William Glock's summer schools at Bryanston, where in 1951 they did the second part of the *Childhood of Christ*, giving Colin his first inkling of the glories of Berlioz's music. It was an experience he has never forgotten, although he was not able to follow up "one of the most marvellous moments of my life" for some years. He did a good deal of conducting at these music schools, which gave him invaluable experience, as he had little confidence in himself. He knew a few works well but as yet he could not deal with those that he did *not* know, and nobody then in senior administrative positions was willing to give him any kind of support or encouragement.

The years 1953 to 1957 were the lean ones. During that time Colin gave lessons in Cambridge, conducted the odd provincial concert, broadcast once or twice with the Kalmar, and with the BBC regional orchestras. That was all. But he stuck at it, which shows just how determined he was to become a conductor, even when he saw instrumental colleagues of his own generation making much quicker progress. He did receive reassurance from having the encouragement of musical non-musicians such as Isaiah Berlin, the late Victor Gollancz, and Arthur Norrington, as well as his friends.

Critic and musicologist Stanley Sadie, who was at Cambridge at this time during the early fifties, well remembers Colin Davis's visit to the University Music Club. For the hardly lavish salary of £70 a year, Colin acted as coach to the club. He visited it once a week during term time and mostly gave instruction and help in ensemble playing. The results were stimulating for all concerned: he had strong views on shaping the music and made his charges think for themselves.

Colin's provincial jobs included being conductor of the orchestral society in Ipswich, of a choir called the Hill Singers in Wimbledon, and of another in Redhill called the Redhill and Reigate Singers. However, the outlook seemed depressing. He thought that if he had no job by the time he was forty, he would disintegrate as a person. The door to small German opera-houses where many young conductors find their way, was closed because he could not play the piano and therefore was not competent to act as a repetiteur. Indeed this was the objection to him as a conductor in the view of many professional musicians: if he was not a pianist, he had no business trying to be a conductor. He could not agree with them because he happened to be conducting. Nor, perhaps, did they feel he had the academic calibre. Right up until today, he does not believe that he has to justify what he does by any kind of academic rule.

❦ BBC Scottish ❦ Orchestra

He applied three times for the post of assistant conductor of the BBC Scottish Orchestra, and finally in 1957 he received the appointment. This was the first turning-point in his career. The third time of asking seemed like his battle of Waterloo. Besides he had received other encouragement from the BBC. He had also taken part in a London Philharmonic Orchestra scheme for young conductors and directed Schubert's *Unfinished* Symphony—apparently at a very slow pace—at Catford Town Hall. That led to a concert at St Pancras Town Hall, which he describes as a total failure on his side. For the most part he had no idea yet how to deal with professional musicians because he had not been brought up in a professional kind of way—"The great English disease of the amateur, if you like" is how he states it, and others confirm the view. That was why the Scottish appointment was so important. Largely out of the glare of the public, he was able to get onto terms with orchestral players, make his mistakes, expand his repertory.

Ian Whyte, who was the orchestra's chief conductor, spent nearly all his time on the standard works so that Colin could try out much of the modern repertory, and make his first real acquaintance with what was soon to be one of his greatest loves—Berlioz. Many of his interpretations at this time were as yet unformed, sometimes wildly wrong, but the very fact that he was able to try them out was of inestimable value. Practically all the conductors who have gone to this particular job in Scotland as either assistant or chief conductor have come out of it having been tried in the fire, toughened and matured by the experience. So did Colin, without losing his essential enthusiasm for love of music. The job taught him what being a conductor was. The players were very nice to him, bearing with him through his triumphs and miseries.

Meanwhile his happy association with the loyal Chelsea Opera Group continued, helping him vastly to widen his operatic horizons. The works included *Freischütz*, *Falstaff*, *Fidelio*, and of course plenty of Mozart. He also was in charge of Nicolai's *The Merry Wives of Windsor* at the Peter Jones Theatre in 1957. So that when the chance came to conduct at Sadler's Wells he was ready for the challenge. Then there was a Festival Hall concert with Clara Haskil, and that famous *Don Giovanni*.

Between these two occasions substituting for Klemperer came a concert

[*Erich Auerbach*

In the pit at Sadlers Wells Theatre during his time as musical director there.

at the 1959 Edinburgh Festival, and it was this—not the Festival Hall *Don Giovanni*, as is commonly supposed—that drew the "Best Since Beecham" comment from *The Observer*. What Peter Heyworth actually wrote on that occasion was as follows: "Mr Davis conducted two works in a manner that showed that he is not only outstanding among our younger conductors but probably the best we have produced since Sir Thomas Beecham, his senior by forty-eight years. In Stravinsky's delicious *Danses Concertants*, he achieved a precision and subtlety of orchestral colour and a melodic grace worthy of an old wizard like Ansermet, but his rhythms had more bite and urgency".

And of Davis's performance of Mozart's *Jupiter*, Heyworth wrote just as encouragingly: "I can only say that I cannot readily recall a performance of the *Jupiter* so totally satisfying as this . . . for me the unique quality of the performance was the manner in which he revealed the music's gravity and substance without ever losing its nimble grace. . . ."

As far as the *Don Giovanni* itself is concerned, Giulini was first invited to take over the performance. He was able to do the records EMI made at the time but not the concert performance. That put Walter Legge, of EMI, and the Philharmonia, in an awkward position. Colin commented "Now Legge used to like a gamble and it tickled him, I think, to put a little known Englishman in front of an international cast to see what would happen."

What *did* happen? *The Times* (then anonymous) wrote: "Mr Davis seized the opportunity of a reading of *Don Giovanni* worthy of the splendid cast that had been assembled and worthy of the glorious score. It was dramatically intense, musically felicitous in tempo, phrasing and nuance, shot through with love and understanding. It will not quickly be forgotten, partly at least because with it Mr Davis emerged as a conductor ripe for greatness." Noël Goodwin of the *Daily Express* spoke of "a chance in a lifetime" and so it proved.

Colin could have been excused if such encomiums had gone to his head; thankfully, as we have noted, he remained sane, with feet firmly planted on the ground however much others would have liked him to take off immediately. None the less he *was* at last established.

All these performances presented Colin with another problem—how to manage singers. There was, in the first place, a great difference between the Chelsea Opera Group, which might spend several weeks preparing what was after all only a concert performance, and Sadler's Wells where he was working with a permanent repertory company and had the difficulty of re-kindling the excitement of the music with artists who sometimes did not see their singing as anything more than a job. Besides, the career of a singer as compared with that of the conductor is short so that the relationship in those days, and even today, for him was often one between a senior and a junior—even if they are the same age. "When people see a young man at the opera house who has just arrived without much experience, throwing his weight about, then naturally they don't like it and I don't blame them. That's why I can say that I really learned how to behave myself at Sadler's Wells."

✣ Sadler's Wells ✣

Before he went to the Wells as musical director, he conducted Mozart's *The Seraglio* with Elizabeth Harwood as a marvellous Constanze (she, too, went on to greater things, taking this part at the Salzburg Festival). That was as early as 1958 when John Warrack recognised, in the *Daily Telegraph*, that "we have a Mozart conductor of the first rank". In the summer of 1960, Colin returned to Glyndebourne, where he had first encountered Mozart opera as a clarinettist, to conduct *The Magic Flute*, replacing an indisposed Sir Thomas Beecham. Although I have happy memories of the performance (not least of Pilar Lorengar's exquisite Pamina and Oliver Messel's decor—still the most satisfying in my memory for this piece) and of Davis's conducting, the Press was mixed. Perhaps Andrew Porter's report in *The Financial Times* was the most apt: "Colin Davis . . . makes the mistake of wanting to go straight to the heart of the matter— whereas the seriousness and sublimity of *The Magic Flute* should take us by surprise. His overture is already ponderous, for the six repeated quavers on which it is built are all given equal weight. His affection for the music is everywhere evident, revealed in choice textures and moulded phrasings. He achieved some marvellous moments . . . but often the tempi were slow and early on in the second act the drama seemed to have stopped." Colin admits that the performance was not entirely a success and has reservations about the work (which we shall come to in a moment). There were also some unhappy circumstances attending the preparation of the work, not altogether of the conductor's making.

The Wells job proved Colin as an operatic conductor in the way the Scottish appointment had done for him as an orchestral one. He could go round the country doing *Carmen*, *The Magic Flute*, *Così fan tutte* or whatever, a dozen times and more without the glare of publicity, finding out how to do them. In retrospect, he feels that he was certainly right to stay with this job and withstand the blandishments of the international career, which could have opened up for him after the *Giovanni* success.

John Warrack, writing in *Opera* for November 1965, just after Colin had resigned from his appointment as Musical Director at Sadler's Wells, commented "I doubt if any of us could have foreseen how much he would do. That he improved orchestral standards is well known; apart from the strengthening of personnel, a sense of corporate musicianship began to show itself increasingly in the Wells performances. This was not

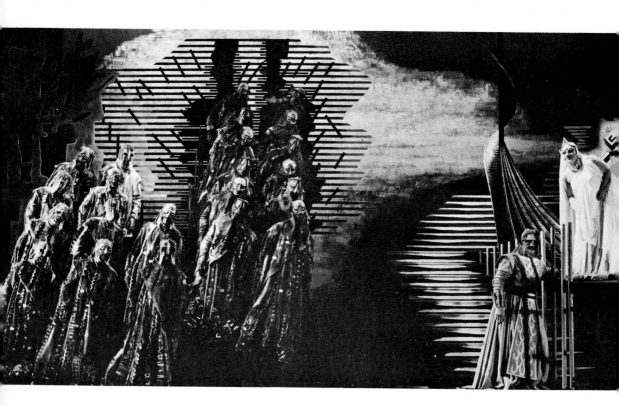

Above: The production of "Oedipus Rex" at Sadlers Wells: The masked men of Thebes listen to Jocasta (Monica Sinclair) and Oedipus (Ronald Dowd) discussing the murder of Laius.

[*Sadler's Wells*

confined to the pit: these were the years when, with an impressive frequency, the Sadler's Wells potential style reached its best—namely a feeling running right the way through from choice of work to designer and producer to casting to orchestral preparation, a feeling that everyone shared, understood and was content with his part in the enterprise. There were disappointments—one of my own most acute, and I later discovered Davis's too, was the Janáček *Cunning Little Vixen*—but against these memory easily produces the highly original *Mahagonny*, *The Rake's Progress*, the stunning *Oedipus Rex* (recorded by EMI), *Idomeneo*, most recently the new *Fidelio*. Even so short a list bears witness not merely to Davis's ability, as a true professional after his own beliefs, to conduct whatever came up (and it takes no account of his *Tosca* and *Tannhäuser* for a start) but to the Wells's interest in expanding the limits of opera that a conventional opera house usually sets . . . .

"As a member of a team that included, as Director of Productions, Glen Byam Shaw and working closely under Norman Tucker with a variety of designers and producers, Davis and his part in all this must not be exaggerated. He has himself expressed worry about the difficulty of being a good administrator as well as a good artist, and certainly the opera house had its normal share of friction in reaching agreement, but friction is the normal way of striking a spark, and Davis's was one of the talents to take fire most easily from ideas that had not at first come naturally to him. What he liked most about Sadler's Wells was 'this sense of working with a team all of whom have come together to do everything possible to improve the standard of performances' . . ."

Right: A scene from "The Mines of Sulphur" at Sadlers Wells with, left to right, Ann Howard as Leda, Gregory Dempsey as Boconnion and Joyce Blackham as Rosalind.

[*SW*

Those who have criticised his Covent Garden appointment on the grounds of his small repertory of operas are inclined to forget just how varied and extensive was his experience at this time. In addition to the works mentioned by Warrack he conducted pieces as different as *Faust*, *La Traviata*, *The Flying Dutchman*, *Ariadne on Naxos*, Pizzetti's *Murder in the Cathedral*, and Richard Rodney Bennett's *The Mines of Sulphur*—hardly a narrow repertory. There was not a Berlioz work among them, although at about this time he recorded *Béatrice et Bénédict* for Oiseau-Lyre.

Also during these years he conducted *Dido and Aeneas* at the Bath Festival (1959) and in 1961 his first Berlioz for the Chelsea Opera Group—*Roméo et Juliette*.

After leaving Sadler's Wells, he had what he describes as "several kicks up the arse", and discovered that the years between 35 and 40 are the great dividing line. Trying to get to grips with the professional world, he did not find a very satisfactory *modus vivendi*. What seemed to matter was how much money you were earning, whether or not you had your interview in the *New York Times*; that sort of thing worried him terribly at the time (but not in later years). He wondered whether he should go into that world to the exclusion of other things or whether one should make forays into it and then retreat, the uneasy balance between a private existence and public life. This was partly the cause of the break-up of Colin's first marriage. He felt, too, that he must have a home, a base, where people are committed to one another.

❧ BBC Symphony ❧ Orchestra

Colin left Sadler's Wells in 1964: when Monteux died it was thought he would become chief conductor of the London Symphony Orchestra. In fact, the job went to Istvan Kertesz. Various other possibilities then offered themselves. The Frankfurt Opera was looking for a musical director and Davis was one of the candidates considered. He went over to conduct *Entführung* (a success) and *Carmen*, which he is convinced the orchestra had decided would be a failure—as it was—and the job went to Theodore Bloomfield. Then one day he met William Glock who suddenly asked him to become Chief Conductor of the BBC Symphony Orchestra. Colin was surprised to say the least, because he felt that at that time Glock was rather sceptical about him. Of course, he accepted the offer. In January, 1965, he was awarded the CBE.

Sir William (as he now is) had known Davis for about 23 years. In fact he can remember playing Mozart's C major Piano Concerto with Colin as conductor as long ago as 1948 at a summer school, and he has en-couraged and advised him ever since. At this juncture in 1965 he felt that the BBC orchestra should have a British conductor and that Colin's en-thusiasm and liveliness would be good for the players who then needed buoying up. It would also be good for Colin to settle down for a while with one orchestra, to help in the administration and the choosing of players. Glock also realised that if he did not engage Davis at this point in his career there would be little chance of ever getting him.

I interviewed Colin at the time of his appointment in December 1965 (although it was only effective from September 1967) and he then des-cribed the post as "the greatest challenge of my life and the completion of my professional education . . . . The opportunities are immense: the or-chestra has the widest repertory of any, both because of its function as a broadcasting orchestra and because sufficient funds are available to make its existence independent of public attendance . . . ."

He felt that he had reached a watershed in his life: "I have turned both my private and my public life upside down and arrived at something new. If that doesn't happen between 30 and 40 it never will. In addition, as you approach 40, passionate emotions simmer down—you get odd and beauti-ful glimpses of objectivity, looking at both people and things, and you observe your own reactions to them".

[*Camera Press*

He hoped to tackle a good deal of new music and also some of the larger

works in the repertory, such as Beethoven's Ninth Symphony that he had so far avoided. And he fulfilled his wishes. He and Sir William worked very harmoniously together, although Colin sometimes got impatient as an administrator, and was worried by the often painful decisions to be made about players. Glock considers there are limitations to Colin's repertory, but that he broadened his outlook at the BBC.

Colin likes tackling new works—he described Harrison Birtwistle's *Nomos* as a "huge prehistoric monster"—but if he is bewildered, as he was by Gerhard's Fourth Symphony, he says so. Sir William said "Above all, he is frank and likes others to be just as frank. He has often said to me 'You haven't said what you are really thinking' ".

Both Sir William and Colin are agreed that the first six months with the orchestra were very difficult. Colin was used to the LSO, with whom he had had an abrasive but stimulating relationship. With the more homely BBC Symphony, he had to learn how to manage people and how to get the best out of them in a different kind of way. He feels that he and the orchestra got on increasingly well and gave some "cracking concerts". One particularly remembered was in Amsterdam, all of Berlioz. Colin thinks that he left the orchestra a more positive body than he found it.

He also managed, after a difficult period, to establish a rapport with the Prom audiences. After Sir Malcolm Sargent died, there was a good deal of resistance to Davis as his successor, because he was a different personality and a younger one who could not play the father figure. Davis accepted the challenge and, in his own right, has been accepted by the 'Prommers'.

Some players think that his technique can be awkward, using too much energy for too small effect. Sir William puts it a little differently, believing

Opposite: Rehearsing for the television production of Berlioz's "L'Enfance du Christ"; [CP

Below, left to right: Rehearsing the BBC Symphony Orchestra—Davis's comment, "You must try not to get intoxicated with the wonderful music. It's marvellous, the power—you sweep your arm down and a gigantic fortissimo comes out".

The Last Night of the Proms, 1967; [BBC

The Last Night of the Proms, 1969; [BBC

that he is apt to make too much of detail at the expense of line. Philip Jones, who was one of the first trumpets with the orchestra during the whole of Davis's chief conductorship, saw his initial problem as one of organisation. He compared it to a man of 40 inheriting a large family with a lot of grown-up children, many of them older than himself, and who then became the boss—"Poppa"—of people around him who have had far more experience of the orchestral business. Jones feels that it took Colin a year completely to assert his authority and come to terms with his "family".

In Jones's view many conductors see conducting as the "grandest occupation", but that Colin is not a bit like that. He prefers to commune with his players, even to philosophise with them, because he feels that a performance is an interpretation that must create something above the mere notes. Some players, the hardened ones, do not always respond easily to this approach, preferring a professionally toughened personality who knocks them about a bit. The system of co-principals at the BBC also meant that players did not always feel part of the orchestra. However, there seems little doubt that over his four years with the orchestra its performances improved immeasurably; and so did its conductor's. The shame of it is that having reached something of a peak with the orchestra, he then had to leave because of the invitation from Covent Garden to become musical director from September 1971, which he could not refuse.

At a BBC rehearsal I found Colin relaxed in the knowledge that he has the ear of his orchestra. Preparing the *Prague* Symphony of Mozart, he runs through the whole work at first, throwing out the occasional word of advice about phrasing or rhythms or expression. The introduction goes

appallingly but Colin does not, at this stage, stop to correct matters; at the end of the first movement he comments wryly: "Let's press on to put as much music as we can between us and the introduction." He seems at once fatherly and brotherly.

Once the run-through is complete, he returns to the introduction and, with scrupulous care, goes over it bar by bar, discussing various points with his strings that seem to be giving difficulty, sorting out problems of balance. The procedure can perhaps best be described by the American phrase "advise and consent", and the results, as can be heard, are miraculous. As Colin put it: "There's no point getting angry with the orchestra if they've played as badly as they did during that introduction because they already *know* they've not brought it off. When I was beginning I probably would have attacked them but I soon came to realise that that approach must be wrong."

As he rehearses the rest, he stops now and again to get a detail right, but by and large he relies on perceptive comments as he goes along, indicating a significant key change here, an important secondary idea there. For the rest he depends, as do so many good conductors, on his eyes, keen and expressive, to give guidance and inspiration, and these eyes seem to typify his combination of true feeling with technical punctiliousness.

International Commitments

During the period 1968 to 1970, Colin's career took on an even stronger international flavour and he was in demand everywhere. The summer of 1968 found him at the Proms, and recording *Idomeneo* for Philips. In the autumn a period with the BBC Symphony was followed by concerts with the Boston Symphony and New York Philharmonic. Back with the BBC in December he was preparing a performance of Berlioz's *Damnation of Faust.* Then he took the Orchestra on a tour of the Benelux countries at the start of 1969. Concerts with the BBC, including a studio recording with the orchestra of *Tristan und Isolde* and a public concert performance of Mozart's *La Clemenza di Tito*, were followed by a period at the Metropolitan Opera, New York, where he directed—with enormous success— *Peter Grimes* and *Wozzeck*, returning to London in May to conduct the Britten opera at Covent Garden. In June he conducted the Berlioz *Requiem* at St Paul's, then appeared at the Bath and Aldeburgh Festivals with the BBC SO.

A three-week holiday was followed by the Proms and then, quite exhaustingly, a new production of Berlioz's *The Trojans* at Covent Garden, running concurrently with the recording of the same work for Philips. Concerts with the BBC SO and LSO in the autumn were succeeded in the New Year 1970 by performances of *Fidelio* (with Gwyneth Jones and Jon Vickers) at Covent Garden and another spell with the Boston Symphony. *Wozzeck* at Covent Garden in April, a month's holiday (in May) and Covent Garden performances of *The Midsummer Marriage*, followed by a recording of the work for Philips, completed a two-year cycle perhaps not untypical of the busy conductor today and probably un-heard of in a pre-war, pre-jet age.

[BBC

❦ Covent Garden ❦

He received just before the Covent Garden offer a tempting one from the United States (the Boston Symphony) but he felt that if he did not accept the opportunity of going to the Royal Opera it might never arise again. He also felt strongly that if Covent Garden wanted him, he *ought* to go there. He considered at this juncture that to go back to the opera house was to face another challenging set of difficulties—and another education; it would "throw me into the ocean of Wagner; otherwise I would wade from the shore and never dive in. I may make a frightful mess of it but at least I shall emerge at the other end as a different person". He also wants to conduct all the great pieces such as *Otello*, *Falstaff*, the major Mozart operas, some Puccini, and many twentieth-century works.

Above all, Colin looks for a kind of special experience in the opera house that will be as far away from routine as possible. He encountered this twice in an opera house—with Glen Byam Shaw as producer at Sadler's Wells and with Peter Hall at Covent Garden. They in their separate ways drew the best out of him as a conductor. When he is able to work together with someone like that everything seems to click from the very first rehearsal. Music and drama at once become fused: they become inextricable.

Such a fusion did not take place in the case of Berlioz's *Les Troyens*, produced at Covent Garden in 1969 with Davis conducting. Upset by what was happening on the stage, he was perhaps unable to give the kind of performance that he simultaneously recorded for Philips. With Tippett's *The Knot Garden* in 1970 and the revivals of *Così fan tutte* and *Peter Grimes* at Covent Garden in 1971 (*Grimes* was also given under him in 1969) the relationship with the producers (Peter Hall and John Copley respectively) and with the singers was so close that Colin was able to complement what he approved of on the stage with his musical performance. That *Così*, at least most of the later performances, was one of his finest achievements to date and not surprisingly it had come in a Mozart work. This was followed by the widely acclaimed *Le Nozze di Figaro*, the first new production of the Davis regime, in December, 1971.

During the 1960s and early 1970s his tours with the LSO and BBC Symphony took him all over Europe, America and the Far East. In the United States he was so admired by the Boston Symphony Orchestra that

Above: Anne Howells (Dorabella) and Robert Kerns (Guglielmo) in the 1971 performances of "Così fan tutte" at Covent Garden.

[*Royal Opera House*

21

Above: Scenes from the premiere of Sir Michael Tippett's opera "The Knot Garden" in 1970.

[ROH

they decided to make him Principal Guest Conductor from the 1972–3 season. In June 1971 he conducted the Berlin Philharmonic with great success and even that most fastidious of orchestras wanted him to return immediately. But Colin decided to divide his time between Covent Garden, Boston, the Proms and recording (he signed an exclusive contract with Philips in 1964), rightly realising that these commitments were more than enough to fill any one conductor's time. Even the Metropolitan and New York Philharmonic had to take second place, although he was reportedly more admired there by the players than any contemporary conductor. Apparently they felt that he neither patronised them nor treated them like children but rather dealt with them like intelligent beings with whom the music could be discussed. Jack Phipps, who is Colin's agent and longtime friend, says that during the past five years or so Colin has learnt how to cope with the problems of guest-conducting famous orchestras and cites the Berlin Philharmonic as an example; his first visit to Berlin in 1962 had not been a particular success. When he returned last June, as we have seen, the players were at his feet.

❧Composers❧

His first love for Mozart came in his clarinet-playing days, and with his early gramophone listening. He used to pore over Mozart's K450 concerto. "We had no electric light of any kind upstairs in our house, and I used to call on the last movement of this work to keep up my spirits in the dark, whistling it on my way. At school I played the Clarinet Quintet, and clarinet-playing in general brought me more and more into contact with Mozart. As a boy, and even as a young man, you're intoxicated with his music. Now I suppose I have begun to see more penetrating detail, and I think you need what he's trying to say much more as you grow older: 'Don't, whatever you do, take yourself seriously, and don't, whatever you do, judge anyone—that's offensive. If you just manage to love them sufficiently, you'll find they're bearable'."

"I suppose I first came into contact with the operas when I played in the off-stage band in *Don Giovanni* under Fritz Busch at Glyndebourne, and once or twice in the pit in *Così fan tutte*. And I listened day after day to the rehearsals of all the Mozart pieces. I was besotted with him then, and I suppose no less so today. He seems more extraordinary than ever to me

Below left: Heather Harper as Ellen Orford, Jon Vickers in the title role of "Peter Grimes" at Covent Garden in 1971.

[ROH

Below: A welcome cup of tea after a performance at Covent Garden.

[CP

as the years go by and I come to understand the operas even more deeply. His extraordinary-ness is not just as a composer—his gift in this respect is so obvious that nobody needs to mention it—but also the atmosphere in which his mind operates is a very healthy one: it is what you might call totally Christian, although it may not appear so insofar as no one is judged and everyone is loved. People's idiosyncracies are laughed out of court and only people who take themselves too seriously, like Don Giovanni, have in fact to be popped into the oven until they see the absurdities of their ways. All this makes for a certain kind of joyfulness which is not, however, untouched by great depths of suffering, but that suffering is embraced in—well, there's no other word—love. In the truest sense he rejoices in the gifts he was granted, and he puts them to the greatest possible use".

One work he has neglected in recent years is *The Magic Flute* because he feels it is a bad piece dramatically, especially in the second act. "To have to return to Papageno after you've been through the trials of fire and water with Pamina and Tamino is all very well, but it does become very protracted. Then some of the numbers are so very short. They're perfect, of course, but to string them along with all that dialogue in between is difficult. With *secco* recitative you stay within the convention; with talk you immediately come out of it. Suddenly you have to create a piece as wonderful as 'Bei Männern' out of nothing. You cannot accumulate tension. Any conductor, if they're telling the truth, will tell you that the task is almost impossible. For me, it doesn't have the same kind of truth as *Figaro*, *Così* and *Don Giovanni*. There he manages to transform every day things by means of music so that you see something extra, but there's nothing every day about a man having his mouth locked up by a padlock, is there?

"In *Figaro*, the marvellous thing is that everything is absolutely true. When the Count and Countess are having a quarrel, they're really quarrelling and though fairy stories can be full of meaning of one kind or another, I find Schikaneder's contribution rather puerile. In the second-act finale of *Figaro*, in the midst of the confusions and disputes, suddenly Mozart writes that marvellous chorale—suddenly it lifts you and shows you the other side of the coin. Mozart seems to be saying—there it is, that's all you're allowed. In the *Flute*, the message is laid out so obviously that you almost miss the point. I'm not trying to destroy *The Magic Flute* —I want to hear the music but I don't particularly want to see it. Similarly with *Titus*, which is like some of the later piano concertos in paring down the notes to the minimum, in a kind of distillation of his style, a curious, almost deliberate sweetening of it. He seems in some senses already old and burnt-out. This gives these works a very touching quality but misses the impact of his earlier operas. You listen to the music but you don't get involved with the people. To return to the *Flute*, I think the attitude there is very different from that in the earlier operas. It seems to teach us less than the more human happenings in the other pieces. It's already a very nineteenth-century opera in the sense that Mozart is now involved with the suffering of his characters rather than looking at them from the outside, and this whole outlook culminated finally in Wagner. In the other works, there is this marvellous balance between not taking oneself too seriously and loving everyone, seeing their foibles but not blinding one to

Opposite page: The performance itself. Geraint Evans as Leporello, Gobbi as Giovanni
[ROH

Discussing a point with Tito Gobbi during rehearsals for "Don Giovanni", 1969
[CP

Kiri Te Kanawa as The Countess and Reri Grist as Susanna in "Figaro," 1971
[ROH

In the conductor's room, Davis greets his wife Shamsi (left) and friends.
[CP

Rehearsing the Royal Opera House orchestra.

[ROH

their good points. If you end in laughter, you cannot have tragedy. *Don Giovanni* could be tragic but Mozart is not going to have it so.

"That twilight feeling I just mentioned doesn't I think apply to the *Requiem*, which has all the ferocity and force of his youth, as well as the new maturity he had found in the *Flute*."

Charles Reid once pointed out just how Davis makes Mozart so real to an orchestra. Colin was once doing a Mozart slow movement and the bar before a bassoon entry he warned: "Here comes the *poison* note. It often happens in Mozart, this touch of poison, this shadow on felicity." The technical point at issue, wrote Reid, was the bassoon's evoking of a tonality and mood remote from the established one; to state the case in terms of key signatures would have been a retreat from reality into the classroom. Certainly I have found in conversation with Colin an almost obsessive desire to avoid the academic in order to concentrate on the meaning of the music. That's what may have drawn him to Berlioz, the least academic of composers.

He knew nothing at all about Berlioz as a boy or even as a young man. The first contact between the two came, as we have seen, at a summer school performance of *The Childhood of Christ*, conducted by Roger Desormière. "This ability of his to spin a line of melody immediately appealed to me—and it still does. What I like about him, I suppose, is that he is still a classical composer, and his feeling of order and innocence perhaps appeals to some of us more than expressive self-indulgence. When there is something objective about the music, we feel happier than when there is something obsessively personal. His world is an extension of that of Mozart, particularly the Mozart of *Idomeneo*, although in Berlioz Mozart's suppressed demons are at large and the nostalgia for a world of lost innocence more painful. Then there is the same balance between melody, harmony, counterpoint, and colour. Of course, their techniques are very different. Berlioz's melodies are unlike everyone else's, and Mozart might have raised his eyebrows at some of Berlioz's harmonic procedures; but I guess he would not have minded having written the Nocturne from *Béatrice et Bénédict*.

"I always compare Blake's vision and his obsession with line, to Berlioz's interest in melody. Both attempt to transcend the material Satanic fact, Blake through Christ, Berlioz through beauty. Blake dreamed of his new Jerusalem, Berlioz of a land, unlike his own, where art would at least be taken seriously. Each would welcome the other in his City of Imagination. Blake has that famous quotation 'The ordinary man sees the sun and says it's like a golden guinea', but when I see the sun, I see thousands of angels saying 'Holy, holy, holy'. That's it—and Berlioz has it too—the double vision."

There is another aspect of Berlioz that means a great deal to Davis and which he expressed thus in an interview with David Cairns. "He's disturbing, isn't he? He doesn't move in a comfortable, logical way from one thing to another. He will sometimes produce so many original effects in such a short time that some listeners won't be bothered with it and say he's being eccentric or just producing a lot of noise.

"You can't get out of Berlioz's music the things you might like to get. It doesn't give you the sensation of a drug. (The second half of *Tristan* is like half-a-dozen reefers). And—this is very curious—it doesn't give you a sense of the classical virtues of order, proportion, and the sense of God being in his Heaven. And his music isn't self-indulgent, even at its most poetic. Nobody can wallow in it—it's far too beautifully wrought for people just to have a good cry or a good sing.

"The other side of that particular coin is his ferocity. When Berlioz is being ferocious, it's like being bashed up and down an alley-way, isn't it? No wonder people who don't want to be disturbed by music can't be bothered with it. Yet if you look at something like the middle section of the *Franc-Juges Overture*, where there's that very poignant tune on the woodwind in semibreves and the most ferocious interruptions in the strings, bass drum and trombone—they seem bent on tearing the fabric of the music to pieces—you find that each one is a four-bar phrase. Unbelievable in Berlioz that it should be so! But it's necessary, otherwise it would fall to pieces. It doesn't sound like four-bar phrases, but that's how it's organised and it's all perfectly clear and worked out. His sense of earthquake and things beyond one's control is perfectly measured, I think."

Davis came to Stravinsky at Bryanston Summer School and, as we have seen, during his time in Glasgow with the BBC Scottish Orchestra. He believes in him as the great figure of our time for his renewal of musical language.

"Take something like the Mass, one of my favourite works; it's so marvellously objective and so beautiful. It's discovering works like that which is exciting. There are still other pieces I want to do and it's this turning to the unfamiliar that offers you most refreshment—or coming back to a piece that you haven't done for donkey's years. You've got older and you see things differently without having lost your enthusiasm for it. In Stravinsky, I think that you feel sanity has been restored after some of the excesses of the late nineteenth century."

A performance of *Oedipus Rex* under Basil Cameron at the Albert Hall was another significant event in Colin's move towards Stravinsky. "This seemed to me to be remarkable. When I was hopelessly out of work in my mid-twenties I studied this piece among others, really every note of it in order to give myself something to do. Then about 1960 I did some of the ballets at Covent Garden. I remember *The Fairy's Kiss* and *The Rite of Spring*."

Noël Goodwin commented on *The Fairy's Kiss* in *Dance and Dancers* (June 1960) that Davis "secured playing of a much higher standard than the Royal Ballet usually brings upon itself," and Oleg Kerensky in the *Daily Mail* wrote that "Colin Davis . . . made one realise how much we suffer from the routine conducting of so many ballets". Eleven years later Colin Davis, now musical director-elect at Covent Garden, returned to conduct some performances of *The Song of the Earth* for the Royal Ballet to equally enthusiastic noises from the Press. Thus it is not surprising that he wanted to work often with the company as well as trying to bring together, as is right and proper, the Royal Opera and Ballet in joint productions of works such as Berlioz's *Roméo et Juliette* and Stravinsky's *Les Noces*. In his role as a ballet conductor he must be as much committed to the music and to the joint effort with the dancers as one is to the score of an opera and the singers. Besides, he likes anything that takes place in the theatre and is involved in it the entire time.

❧ *Philosophy* ❧
of Life

Work in the opera house means organization as much as music-making and Colin, with his awareness of time, is bored and annoyed by the hours spent on petty matters that could be better devoted to music. Likewise, he believes that musicians are set apart in the sense that they do not lead ordinary lives from a time point of view. "Music is a kind of escape from time and because of this musicians' lives seem to go so terribly fast. As you're not living time in the ordinary sense, the day seems to be gone in a flash, and it's difficult to find out what has actually happened to it."

One point he likes about being a conductor is having responsibility for people with whom he actually comes into contact. "You know everyone in your organisation and it's very salutary to meet them all the time. The orchestra, chorus, opera house or whatever is your kingdom and you know the people in it—and that's very unusual today."

He does not believe that his job, or that of the opera house, or that of the symphony orchestra are going to cease to exist in the near future. People are going to need more music not less, although with many of his contemporaries, particularly conductors, he is concerned about the way some composers are moving away from writing for these institutions as we have known them until now. Not that he is a reactionary; he likes the music of Tavener, Birtwistle, Maxwell Davies among others, but he cannot get on with the avant-garde as represented by Stockhausen and his disciples. He is honest enough to recognise that much of what is being written is simply too difficult for him to conduct "without learning a whole new vocabulary of gestures, and there is a point where you get too old to learn. You explore up to the age of 45 and then you leave it to other, younger people. Klemperer was experimenting in Berlin back in the 1920s, but today he is content to conduct what he knows. In any case, there is a great deal I still have to tackle in the standard repertory—from Bach to Janáček—that I feel I should concentrate on learning this. One doesn't have such a passion, when one reaches a certain age, to do a particular new piece. One does what comes along. One is more obviously a professional and takes a more general view of music. Perhaps it becomes a less personal thing."

Then he feels that there is so much to get to know or hear again in other musical worlds, such as chamber music. "The first movement of Mozart's C major Quintet, the slow movement of the *Hammerklavier*—

*Above: Colin with his two sons
by his second marriage.*
[*Michael Evans*]

*Above right: Studying a score at
home.*
[*CP*]

these worlds that exist and which we as practising musicians in another
field never have enough time to explore. As an active artist, perhaps just
listening is more difficult, and it can be a colossal shock when one has been
at music all day to hear—passively—something like a Beethoven quartet.
It can be a marvellous influence."

Away from music, he spends a great deal of time reading—"things that
say what I want them to say. There are five books that have recently
seemed to me to be worthwhile. Two are by Hermann Broch, *The Sleep
Walkers* and *The Death of Virgil*. Then there's a man called Hesse, who
wrote *Stephan Wolf* and *The Glass Bead Game*, the last three poetical
novels. Then *Odyssey* of Kazantzakis is a tremendous book. These have
helped me to come to terms with the situation we are all in. They're
about the same thing really, which is that we live in the crack between two
civilisations, and that this is just about the most uncomfortable time
possible. You can see symptoms of it in everyone's behaviour, if you care
to look.

"Our tradition is dying off and we don't know what's going to happen
after it. All we treasure is in a sense long since dead. What is being thrown
up now is uncertain and we don't know where it's going. Everything is in
such a turmoil, practical matters and religion as well as music, painting
and writing. Broch takes Virgil as the example of a man who lived at the
end of Roman times and just before the birth of Christ he says: 'What we
have is gone and what is to come is not yet', and this is an examination of
his situation and why he tried to destroy the Aeneid. And he comes to the
conclusion that what he would have liked to have done was to make one
useful gesture towards this appalling impasse instead of dabbling in
poetry and pleasing himself.

"Hesse's *The Glass Bead Game* is a fantasy about the next millennium, in
which there's no longer any creative work at all but there's a profound
scholarship and this game played is with certain formulas, which have
been abstracted from works of art—a melody by Berlioz or a line by
Shakespeare—and they play this game to get new relationships. The book

Above: Shamsi, Colin and son Kurosh in 1966.

[Alfred Eisenstaed

is about a man who becomes the master of this game, and again wants to make one significant human gesture, so he leaves his exalted position in the tiny state, which is devoted to an intellectual elite, and goes to be a tutor of a boy, and is immediately drowned.

"Kazantzakis's great thing is the conversion of matter into spirit. What you have to do is to cheat death by living to such an extent that when Death finally comes to collect you there's nothing left. It's easy to call these books pretentious; but if nobody attempts any kind of synthesis, if no one tries to attempt to sort out what people are going through, then everything in life became pointless.

"People used to have a place in society. A village was a unit and each person knew what his job was. You were useful. Now we have nothing to attach ourselves to, and we have no psychological framework. Heaven, Hell and Redemption are no longer beliefs held by the vast majority of people. I sometimes wonder whether my little boys are going to be able to manage. Will the healing have begun by the time they're our age, or are they going down to a real doom. If I'd lived a few hundred years ago, I would be a staunch member of the church, but I can't today because the church cannot do what I want it to do—it has run out of juice. I can do it with Mozart—I can sing *Kyrie Eleison* with him and mean it because I know what I'm saying, but I can't do it in church".

Earlier in his own life he attempted to educate himself ("after I'd left school"). Then he read all the Russians but now feels that the great novels of the nineteenth century are too remote; "It's now that we need help desperately. The last century merely plots our downfall: you can follow it to where we are now. I suppose it really began with the Reformation, and the breakup of the church's power, and the beginning of science. Broch shows how each faculty is pursued for its own sake—relentlessly and logically, which means that you drive infinity further and further away. Where God used to be, there, firmly in infinity, he has been driven out and finally there isn't anything. After all, we drive music as far as it will go; maybe the analogy is of the sun breaking up into separate planets,

Raimund Herincx as King Fisher in Tippett's "The Midsummer Marriage" at Covent Garden, 1970
[Phonogram

but anyway the connection between things was lost. This comes in *The Sleep Walkers*. There is running through this a thesis on the decline of values. This has certainly made me understand how all this has happened".

How has this pattern of reading and thought affected his music-making? If he can understand what is happening, why people are in such a muddle, he can perhaps see the point of the usefulness of music. Wondering what he was musician for, indeed why he was alive—something you come to at about the age of 35 or over—you look round for something to make sense of it all, and this idea of making a useful, human gesture, found in these books, enabled him to see what he was trying to do. "My business is to be useful. It doesn't matter at all what I or you think about a particular performance. What does matter is, has it been of some help to someone? I'm not here to enjoy myself, or to be self-indulgent, or to think how much money I can make, but to try to make those for whose lives I'm responsible less appalling in the present human predicament. This means that I have to see people in that light and not as obstacles in the way of musical ambitions. This is what keeps me going today. Whether I'm a great or even a good conductor doesn't worry me in the slightest and is not the point. However, if I can get a choir of 250 interested in Mozart's *Coronation Mass* or the Berlioz *Te Deum*, and try to show them what it's about, and to get them to express for themselves what it can mean, to get them to sing *Kyrie Eleison* as though they meant it, I've done something useful. Whether your colleagues say it was no good, or a great performance, or someone says I don't know what I'm doing, has no importance at all, because it's what it's about that matters to me. I can justify myself if those people with whom I'm working can express themselves when I'm in front of them. If I bully them or frighten them—the traditional way of doing it—that's not useful, that's making them regress. People who want God the Father to be in charge of them are forgetting their own responsibilities. Mind you, a lot of people want to be frightened because that gives them security. Beecham got people to do things for him without treating him as God the Father. They knew he was a tremendous old so-and-so who was cheating them half the time, but they didn't mind because he somehow made them feel they were doing something worth while. One's business is to get out of people what they have to give—and get them to give it willingly".

Many of these ideas, particularly the one about re-discovering ourselves before we can build again, bring him into close association with Sir Michael Tippett, whose music he has done so much to bring to the fore. It has been expressed thus, "All things fall and must be built again; do it with joy". Colin first heard *A Child of Our Time* in Central Hall, Westminster, some twenty years ago. Then he conducted it at music camp, and heard the Second Symphony broadcast. However, it was not until he was in a position to do something about it, that he really became immersed in it. He was at first bewildered by *The Midsummer Marriage*, but after hearing the broadcast under Norman Del Mar he tried to persuade Sadler's Wells to do it. When David Webster wanted to do it at Covent Garden again, Colin was the obvious choice.

However, it is Tippett as a person who means so much to Colin. "There are not enough people like him. Too much of the time I find only mis-understanding: people are indulging themselves when they think they are feeling and academic when they imagine they are thinking. Michael has a fine mind, and it's of use to him because of what he does with it in his music, which is about something. People who write music about music, if you see what I mean, are pointless".

Tippett himself is very frank about Davis's relationship with his music. "He came into it on his own at that performance of *A Child of Our Time*. He thought this was something very precious, and he hoped it wasn't going to die tomorrow. There was undoubtedly something that pulled him towards both the person and the music. But this came to something only when he heard Del Mar's performance of *The Midsummer Marriage*, and this swept him into it so then he felt that he must get into touch with it. Then I got to know him and put my absolute trust in him as a conductor of my music. When it came to *The Knot Garden* I left him entirely in charge—I simply will not interfere with how someone is conducting my work, but anyway I know that Colin has an instinctive understanding of what I want without our ever having discussed it. I just feel he's the tops where interpreting my music is concerned. I certainly prefer him to myself in my own works".

Joan Carlyle as Jenifer, Alberto Romedios as Mark in Act 3 of Tippett's "The Midsummer Marriage" at Covent Garden.

[Phonogram

Tippett speaks of Colin's deep inner life and his semi-religious feelings, and of their mutual understanding of that part of life. Colin himself summed it up thus: "Tippett's is an entirely individual voice and his music stems from his relationship with his own psyche. Surely this is why he writes his own librettos; to use another's would allow an impossible intrusion into this relationship; it is Blake who cries 'I must create a system or be enslaved by another man's...' Those men who, like Tippett, have tried to express inward experiences have either had to disguise their meaning under a superficially attractive facade or lay themselves open to the charge of attempting to express the inexpressible. Tippett has borrowed from every mythology, psychology, and esoteric tradition, and since all myths come from a central pool of psychological knowledge, the confusion is only apparent".

Colin's philosophic attitude is probably not to the liking of many of the musicians with whom he comes into contact. They are concerned only to understand his beat, receive decided tempi. For them his inner life is irrelevant to his music-making, but it seems to me that he is the kind of person for whom the two things are inextricably linked. He is un-English to the extent that he wants to express what's inside him in some tangible, understandable form rather than merely keeping it bottled up inside for the sake of a stiff upper-lip attitude. On the other hand, away from his music-making, many find that a further contact with him is difficult, possibly because he is not interested in the small talk of artists. Indeed, all his life he has probably not been an easy "mixer" but rather a lone man, anxious to communicate—and, as he says, "be useful"—through his music.

He believes that we cannot always be exactly what we are; we have to compromise but in doing so we must not lose that innocence we had in childhood. Even the hardboiled orchestral musician is as tender underneath his exterior hide, if he did but know it. "Half of us builds a wall round the other half, but this wall of pretence must not be allowed to hide our real selves, and above all in our music-making we must present our real self or it all means nothing."

❧ *The Records* ❧

BERLIOZ

[*Phonogram*

We have already seen how Davis came to know and admire Berlioz, and there seems little doubt that his name will be connected with the French composer's for the rest of his career simply because there is nobody else about who approaches Colin's sympathy with, and intimate knowledge of, Berlioz's scores. I do not think it would be taking the name of the dead in vain to say that not even Sir Hamilton Harty or Sir Thomas Beecham would have been able to rival Colin in comprehensiveness in this field. Comparisons between their respective interpretations would not only be odious but also virtually impossible because of the limited amount of Berlioz recordings the earlier conductors made. However, although Harty and Beecham were in their different ways fighters for Berlioz, neither of them won the day in quite the sense that Davis, with the help of the gramophone, has succeeded in doing. Indeed, when I came to listen to all Colin's records of Berlioz, I was staggered by the amount of Berlioz's music he has already committed to disc. When his *Benvenuto Cellini* and *The Damnation of Faust* have come into the catalogue, he will have recorded all the major works, apart from *Lélio*, and most of the minor ones.

Having heard or re-heard all these performances over a very short space of time, I was particularly struck by the utter consistency of Colin's approach, right from *L'Enfance du Christ*, made for Oiseau-Lyre, in October 1960 down to the big Philips sets recorded over the past two or three years. That consistency is borne out by memories of 'live' performances throughout the 1960s when his Berlioz reputation was being established, first with the Chelsea Opera Group, then with the LSO, then in New York (a Lincoln Center series with the New York Philharmonic) and finally at Covent Garden.

A sympathy for and understanding of a composer's music is hard to express in words. Colin, as we have seen, has spoken of Berlioz's feeling for order and innocence, of the balance between melody, harmony, counterpoint and colour, and of the "double vision" he shares with Blake. Something else seems to emerge from a close study of Berlioz as seen through Davis's eyes and ears: his insight into Berlioz's creation of forms that suit the composer's intellect and musical style. None of Berlioz's major works conforms to given moulds, and Davis seems to have an instinctive feeling for the way Berlioz's mind is going so that he can follow the shape those huge, sometimes even rambling, works are taking without losing sight of the larger vision. This empathy expresses itself in Davis's ability to shape the long, sinuous, sensuous melodies for which Berlioz is noted and to control those sudden shafts of original musical thought that, until recently, so upset many musicians. When you hear what Davis does with that much underrated but somewhat immature piece, *Cléopatre*, which shocked the conservative, uncomprehending fathers of French music, you cannot think that Berlioz is the least eccentric. Davis has grasped that already here a great "original" is at work, yet an "original" who is still very much in the mainstream of nineteenth-century music.

In his recording of the *Symphonie Fantastique*, there is a sense of the order of a classical form being maintained even when it is being put at the service of a broad, vivid Romantic mind. Davis—here as in a wonderful Festival Hall performance, also with the LSO—does not play the work as virtuoso showpiece nor does he exaggerate the fantastic elements. He reminds us how astonishing this work must have seemed in 1830, and still does in many respects today, while preserving its proportions. In short, he is true to the score as a whole and in detail. His is the only recording of the work that I know of to include the repeats in the first *and* fourth movements. A cornet is used, usually, in the waltz. It is also faithful to tempo and dynamic markings, a feature of so many of Colin's records.

The whole performance is so clear and forthright, with very precise detail. The string sforzandi in the introduction, those extraordinary chords at the end of the opening movement, the bells and pizzicato in the Witches' Sabbath are given peculiar vividness. I do not minimise the part of the LSO, at the height of its powers, in helping Davis to achieve this direct interpretation, but the conductor must take the honours, as he does so often elsewhere, for managing to create in the recording studio the intensity and elan of a concert-hall reading. He succeeds, too, in the slow movement, taken very deliberately, in catching the mixture of sadness and serenity, something like a Claude painting, which surely is what Berlioz intended. The clear balance of the recording helps here, although it is not among Philips's best.

Similar qualities inform the recording with Menuhin of *Harold in Italy*. In the elegiac Serenade one again marvels at Davis's ability to evoke the Berlioz timbre and colouring. Before that, at the beginning of the Pilgrims' March, Davis obtains a real *ppp* from the strings when they first intone the *canto*. In the Brigands' march, he matches the lithe vigour and acuteness of attack in Berlioz's writing. His judgement of tempo is superb throughout, especially in the main allegros of the March and Orgy, which must seem fast yet be steady enough to ensure clarity in passages of rapid articulation.

The soloist in this work is Menuhin. As Deryck Cooke put it in *The Gramophone* he "plays the viola as if it were his chosen medium, appearing just as great an artist on it as he is on the violin. He makes full use of the opportunity provided by Davis's dead-sure control of the tempo to deploy his intense *espressivo* to magical effect; and he, too, achieves a ravishing *pianissimo*, not least in the *sul ponticello* arpeggio accompaniments in the *Pilgrims' March*, which sounds for once not like exercises but like the fascinating impressionistic background it really is." This is cer-

[*Phonogram*

A scene from "Les Troyens" at
Covent Garden with Jon Vickers,
centre, as Aeneas.

[Houston Rogers

tainly the most worthwhile performance of the work in the catalogue,
and the EMI recording ideally holds the balance between soloist and
orchestra, even catching the distant throbbing of the violas in the coda of
the Serenade.

Davis is one of the few conductors since Beecham to pay attention to
the neglected concert overtures, *Roman Carnival* apart. Even he does not
conduct them very often in the concert hall so that his record of five of
them is invaluable. *Franc-Juges* is given a splendid performance, catching
the music's youthful high spirits and aplomb. That middle section mentioned in his talk with Cairns above, does truly have a "sense of earthquake and things beyond one's control". The poignant woodwind tune
phrase broken by strings, bass drum and trombone and the menacing
introduction do really seem inspired by the "fires of Hell" as Berlioz
intended. The famous second subject (some may remember it as BBC
TV *Monitor*'s signature tune) is given an easy, airy lilt by Davis. Indeed,
the whole is as good an illustration of Davis's command of Berlioz's
swiftly changing moods; it is an astounding piece if you think that it was
written in 1826 and here you feel its full originality.

King Lear, which dates from 1831, is nearly as remarkable as a work and
as an interpretation. The cellos' motif, representative or not of the King
himself, sounds regally impressive here and the Cordelia–oboe tune
emerges as really heartrending. The sombre texture of the whole, its
exploration of the play's ethos rather than its characterisation, is well
conveyed in this powerful interpretation.

Waverley, an unjustly forgotten piece, is again astonishing for its time
(1826/7). Even at this early stage of his career Berlioz's melody had its
individual shape: the languid cello tune, and its typically striking ac-

companiment on the timpani, could only have come from his pen. Here it is eloquently played and clearly balanced with the wind. By contrast, the allegro has an almost Weberian cut—Berlioz was, of course, a great admirer of Weber. The coda, however, is pure Berlioz. Everything, speeds, balance, and dynamic contrasts, are neatly judged by Davis, who obviously enjoyed as much as Beecham rescuing this kind of exuberant piece from oblivion. In the sorrowful Adagio introduction to the Byron-inspired *Corsair*, Davis again secures really *pp* playing from the LSO strings, and he generates proper excitement in the bustling Allegro. *Carnival Romain* is a little detached and stiff.

[*Phonogram*

The last record of purely instrumental music, chiefly devoted to *Symphonie funèbre et triomphale*, is a magnificent one. The power of this solemn, majestic music is amply transmitted in Davis's reading. This apotheosis of the military band might not seem very well suited to the gramophone; it was written for performance not merely in the open, but also on the march, and Berlioz himself was at the head of the troops conducting as he went. In practice rather than theory it works better today on record than outside, where there are so many other noises to contend with. This recording, made in Wembley Town Hall, manages to give a very good sense of perspective. The noble Funeral March never flags, and the tender oboe tune sings out clearly from the melee. The shattering chords at the beginning of the Funeral Oration leap out of the loudspeaker and the trombone solo, richly played by Dennis Wick, is appropriately lugubrious. The finale, though on a lower plane of invention, still exalts our hearts as it did Wagner's.

However, perhaps the most remarkable piece on this record, which also includes the little prelude Berlioz wrote for *The Trojans at Carthage* when it was performed without *The Fall of Troy*, is the Funeral March for the Final Scene of *Hamlet*. This tragic movement, written in 1848, reflects—as Berlioz intended it should—the "nothingness of life". Its melody and harmony are harrowing "dominated", as Cairns puts it, "by a grinding, persistent rhythm", yet there is a certain grandeur in the gloom, at least until the final deathly hush. The music's full import is conveyed in a performance by Davis and the LSO that is frighteningly urgent and, in those closing bars, emptied of all emotion.

In Berlioz's *Roméo et Juliette*, a "dramatic symphony" as he called it, Davis has a commanding grasp of what the composer was about, an opera-in-the-mind, an ideal fusion of words and music without the necessity for stage action. Berlioz may have been making a virtue of necessity but he succeeded, and Davis succeeds too as his interpreter, in re-enacting Shakespeare's poetry and drama in another idiom. From that thrilling *fugato*, which so graphically suggests the desperate family feuds, to the nobility of the final chorus, Davis manages to keep the total vision in mind while never losing his eye for detail or the excitement of the moment. The Prologue is pregnant with doom and foreboding, lightly brushed aside by the party music. The strophes, warmly sung by Patricia Kern, are touching, and Robert Tear conveys the scepticism of the Mab scherzetto.

"Roméo alone" and the "Love Scene" gain immeasurably from being heard in context. In the first, Davis judges the changes of speed well and he is ever alive to the surging undercurrents in the score—the cellos and

basses at the beginning of "Roméo alone" and the timps under the oboe solo in the same movement. The rapture of the "Love Scene" is suggested by the *Innigkeit* of the playing rather than by more overtly romantic means. One could describe bar by bar how tender, beautiful, gently erotic is this music as here interpreted, but that would be tedious; better to hear the records.

The Mab Scherzo is not taken too quickly; delicacy is to the fore, not bravura. Juliette's Funeral Cortège moves forward with a sad, inevitable tread. The string octaves at the end, an intense crescendo and diminuendo, are marvellously keen and palpitating. Roméo's desperation is clearly depicted at the start of the next section. Then the calmer mood of the Invocation is rudely shattered by the frenzied, dying embrace of the lovers. The performance here is beyond reproach. Some of us might have liked the work to end here—Friar Laurence and the rest can seem something of an anti-climax—but Davis's sense of dramatic situation and the fine singing of John Shirley-Quirk with the orchestra avoids a feeling of let-down. My enthusiasm for this set is unbounded, as I hope I have conveyed.

Next we come to the operas proper. Some seven years separate the recording of *Béatrice et Bénédict* for Oiseau-Lyre and *Les Troyens* for Philips, yet in no sense, except size, is the earlier performance overawed by the latter. The Shakespeare opera stands, I suppose, in relationship to the Virgil one as *Falstaff* does to *Otello* in Verdi's output, and love of the lighter pieces does not in any way diminish respect and admiration for the more heroic ones.

Davis's interpretation of Berlioz's *Much Ado* opera was well summed up by Alec Robertson in *The Gramophone* when he said that he "seemed wholly identified with the orchestra, as if the score was singing within him." This identification mirrors Berlioz's sympathy for the two pairs of lovers. On the stage the work may not have much dramatic point— Somarone always seems a bore, and the omission of the sub-plot leaves a rather bland remnant behind—but with only the music, divorced from the dialogue, to hear, the score can be cherished for its lovely music alone.

Davis catches the romance and warm, summery feeling of the overture, which Hugh Macdonald in his note to the set calls "an amazingly homogeneous patchwork of at least seven extracts from the opera". The languishing accents of Hero's aria, the light, bantering tone of the duet for Beatrice and Benedict, the ardour of Benedict's aria are all there in direction, singing and playing. The *morceau choisi* of the work, however, is the lovely Nocturne for Hero and Ursula, most tenderly sung here by April Cantelo and Helen Watts. The Duke of Weimar said to Berlioz that he must have composed it "by moonlight in some romantic spot"; in fact he sketched it while listening to a speech by a colleague at the Institute. Here joy and sorrow are closely linked as the pair sing of the "Night, serene and calm". Davis and his singers find true inspiration in evoking this moment of enchantment and the number is properly the centre of the work. The tempo in this rocking six-eight is just right.

Davis revels in the quirky instrumentation—guitars, tambourine and trumpets—of the drinking song (No. 9). Beatrice's scena (No. 10) is the most arresting piece in the score. Her "Il m'en souvient" is worthy of the composer of Dido's music. Indeed the fourth act of *Les Troyens* is never far from one's mind in this music, and Davis realises this, giving proper weight and intensity to the chromatic harmony and the individual orchestration. The affinity with *Les Troyens* is all the more marked because the singer here is Josephine Veasey, who is also Davis's Dido. Her luscious, sensuous tone is absolutely right both for the eloquent strains of the aria proper and for the dramatic final section. The finale, a Scherzo-Duettino —to quote Macdonald again—"sets the seal on this most delicate of operas"; Beatrice and Benedict, and Davis, "capture the fleeting spirit of love against the tripping rhythms that began the overture". The youthful Davis seems perfectly attuned to this entrancing music, and once again he captures the spirit of a 'live' performance in the studio; in fact, this set was made at the same time as virtually this cast had given a concert reading of the work in the Festival Hall.

Ten years ago, a recording of *Les Troyens* seemed little more than a dream in the mind of that ardent band of Berlioz enthusiasts. Record companies, to whom the idea was mentioned, threw up their hands in dismay at the prospect of investing in a very doubtful product. Who would buy such a huge set? Was Berlioz really as popular as his advocates imagined?

During the 1960s the climate of opinion changed. The enthusiasts grew into a very large company of supporters, and Colin Davis's concert performances were proving that he was very much the man for this mammoth task. In the mid-sixties, he gave several outstanding concert performances of each part separately, and then an overwhelming Prom performance of the whole work. Soon after, it was scheduled for a new production at Covent Garden to consolidate the pioneering task of Rafael Kubelik and John Pritchard in the previous production, which itself had shown the work, contrary to received opinion, more than viable

as a stage performance. The success of the *Ring* recordings, incidentally, showed that the public was in fact ready to purchase large sets at full price. Further encouragement came from the publication, by Bärenreiter, of an authoritative, accurate edition of the score.

At first, it was EMI which was to record the work, the initiative coming from Peter Andry, chief of its International Artists' Department, who at the beginning of 1968 set up the recording for the following year in Walthamstow Town Hall. However, by now Davis was under contract to Philips, and David Cairns, one of the chief architects of the recording, was also soon to be employed by that company. Eventually conflicts were resolved and the recording plans were taken over by Phonogram (today's company name for Philips records).

The sessions began two days after the first night at Covent Garden (September, 17, 1969) and continued for the next five weeks. The advantages of being able to take over a fully rehearsed stage production were somewhat diminished by the inevitable strain the heavy schedule placed on Colin, his singers, and the Royal Opera's chorus and orchestra. As the producer, Erik Smith said to me: "The pros and cons are about equally balanced. There's no doubt that the involvement and tautness Colin and the cast achieved throughout was made possible only because he could return to the opera as a whole every few days. Against that was the fact that the recording schedule was sometimes in jeopardy because of the sheer physical strain imposed on everyone in their double tasks over a whole month."

What does the work mean to Colin? "*The Trojans*, like *Idomeneo* or the *Matthew Passion*, is one of the few noble pieces in the repertory. That's why it's particularly precious. It appeals to us because, in a context of fate and suffering that we sense to be true, it restores human life to dignity and grandeur." And in the booklet that goes with the set he adds: "He [Berlioz] felt at home in a world where men were called to obey 'the high command of Jove', where in submission to destiny they found their heroic qualities, and where, rage as they might 'against the dying of the light', death was accepted without self-pity.

"Musically this world is expressed by Berlioz in classical form. Recitative, aria and ensemble are there; melody reigns supreme; feeling is exalted above action. Dramatically, he attempts the different levels of experience with the freedom of juxtaposition that he found in Shakespeare. The personal is exposed beneath the collective and everything driven by the wheels of destiny."

In the very first bars Davis puts us in the picture, which he describes himself as "the Trojans, like lemmings, hurtling to the abyss". His ever-present rhythmic drive can be heard in the whole of the first part; so can his care for the minutiae, such as the very marked accents in the introduction to Cassandra's first entry. Opinions may differ about the casting in this set of that taxing, awkward role; there can be no denying that Davis creates the "nervous intensity" of which he himself speaks. Side 3 brings us Jon Vickers's vivid, if uneven Aeneas, and the ensuing ensemble, "Châtiment effroyable", where as Colin hopes "the blood will freeze in each of our uncomprehending hearts, as it does in those of the Trojans . . . and equally without doubt we shall take the very action which will seal our destruction."

The Trojan March is excitingly handled by Davis and the engineers. There is a very realistic feeling here, an almost tangible sense of the theatre, as the fatal horse enters. Then the sudden halt in the procession strikes fear into the listener as it does into the Trojans.

In the next scene Hector's ghost is vividly conjured before us by that extraordinary introduction and the chromatically descending vocal line. Davis screws up the tension by his insistence on absolute precision and his almost daemonic drive. The Shade himself is sung with great authority by one of France's few notable singers today—Roger Soyer. His Narbal in part two is no less effective. But the scene, one of the most original in all opera, belongs to Berlioz and to Davis, who here as throughout this 'half' of the work realises what Cairns calls the "austere, electric, possessed" sound quality. It is heard, too, in the whole of the final scene of the second act, where the Trojan Women, led and inspired by Cassandra, commit suicide to avoid a fate worse than death. The tone here is appropriately hypnotic, even exalted. That final, minor chord, however, is desperate, tragic.

The opening of *The Trojans at Carthage*, as Davis realises, takes us into a completely different world, one of prosperity, apparent calm and confidence. The mood is broken only when Aeneas arrives to a minor version of the Trojan March. In Davis's words: "There is a quiet, remote fifth in the orchestra as, with a sickening twist of the entrails, Dido realises that her destiny is linked with that of the strangers, and the audience senses that the outcome of this intrusion will be tragic: once again a woman will be sacrificed to the ambitions of a man chosen for greater deeds than love; and it is in Dido's development from widowhood through awakening love, consummation, betrayal, and rage to acceptance and extinction that Berlioz surpasses himself."

Cairns describes the sound quality of this 'half' as "lyrical, sensuous, sun-drenched, star-laden", and again Davis supplies the right timbre. The action moves from the general happiness depicted in the first aria and chorus through the enchanting duet for Dido and her sister, where the latter senses something lacking in Dido's life, through the Royal Hunt and Storm, given a particularly accurate performance in point of speed and dynamics, to the great Quintet, Septet and Duet that lie at the centre of this work, its fourth act in fact. Indeed, the passage from Iopas's song through to the end of the act remains for me, and I am sure many others, the most sustainedly luxuriant music in all Berlioz. Some have felt that Davis does not allow himself to luxuriate enough on this recording; although I can imagine a more poised account, the one we have here fits in well with Davis's total conception. What worries me is that he allowed Vickers's sometimes rough singing to pass. For all his commitment Vickers too often sounds uncomfortable and strained. The recording throughout this wonderful music matches the mellowness of the sound Davis obtains from his orchestra.

He confesses a particular affection for Hylas's song at the beginning of the fifth act: "It balances the mute appearance of Andromache in the first act: both pieces are interludes which show us the sacrifice of ordinary individuals caught up in destinies greater than their own. Hylas, balanced on the top-mast of his ship, is a homesick sailor singing of his childhood home which, as two soldiers point out drily, he will never see again. His

[*Phonogram*

41

Discussing a recording point
[*Phonogram*

mother's arms that rocked him as a child become identified with the sea, and we become aware of the profound desire, which lies at the bottom of our minds, for the final security of death. Hylas falls asleep before he has finished his song: it vanishes, the sigh of a spent soul leaving 'not a rack behind'. Here Berlioz is truly Shakespearian. He has crystallised a universal feeling, briefly with the utmost economy of means. The gentle swell of the music carries us back to the holy moments of childhood and we sense in the words of Hermann Broch, 'that extraordinary oppression which falls on every human being when, childhood over, he begins to divine that he is fated to go in isolation and unaided toward his own death'."

Certainly Dido goes unaided to her death, suffering the anguish of desertion and loneliness. She becomes a tragic heroine and Berlioz, aided here superbly as throughout by Veasey and Davis, evokes all the starkness of her situation in the two final scenes. In the accompanied recitative "Dieux immortels!" and the noble, grief-laden "Je vais mourir" all concerned rise to inspired heights and crown this memorable recording of a masterpiece. As John Warrack commented at the end of his review in *The Gramophone*: "With the work worthily published, performed and now recorded, there is cancelled a debt that has lasted a hundred years".

Of Davis's choral recordings of Berlioz, the *Grande Messe des Morts* —in Westminster Cathedral—has obviously been the most significant undertaking. Berlioz wrote: "If I were threatened with the destruction of all my works save one, I would crave mercy for the *Requiem*". Perhaps it is not a work ideally heard on the gramophone, but Philips have done it proud in this recording. They have achieved the spaciousness it so much demands and, in his direction, Davis has given the music time to breathe. Unlike some of his predecessors, he lets it unfold at a steady, unforced tempo that adds to the sense of majesty and grandeur, and emphasises Berlioz's wish to portray a reborn golden age. This spaciousness and timelessness is, of course, enhanced by the long reverberation period of the cathedral acoustic and the Philips team has seen to it that the 'audience' feel right in the centre of the work: the sound is all-enveloping yet never coarse or over-loud.

In the *Dies Irae*, Davis brings out that "screwing-up of tonality" described by David Cairns in the accompanying booklet and the tremendous brass fanfares in *tuba mirum* sound as they should—an unleashing of super-human forces. In the *Rex tremendae*, Davis understands Berlioz's vision of the abyss while not forgetting the consolation of *qui salvandos* and *salva me*. The almost uncontrolled writhing of the nine-eight at the beginning of the *Lacrymosa* makes one want to jump out of one's seat and pace the room, so horribly vivid is it, and there is the utmost intensity at this movement's *fortissimo* climax. I think Colin recognises here again the startling originality of the music. Surely in 1837, these tearing, abrupt sounds must have stirred people in their seats as much as innovators do today, probably more so.

The quieter, more intimate numbers, which alternate with the big, dramatic ones, come off just as well: the desolation of *Quid sum miser*; the hypnotic repetition of the three notes by the chorus in the *Offertorium* around which Berlioz weaves one of his richest string textures; the plea to God coming from on high and low (flutes and trombones in unison) in the *Hostias*; the magical intrusion of the cymbals in the repeat of the

Sanctus; the extraordinary series of tonic chords, *piano* on the wind and echoed by the violas, at the start of the *Agnus dei*. The performance is not quite faultless: the tone of the tenors is consistently under-nourished, and this section sometimes wavers in pitch; in general the choral sound could with advantage have been more overwhelming. I wonder why the LSO Chorus was not augmented by another, perhaps professional group. Still, this is by a long chalk the most successful version of the work in the catalogue.

There is also some strained male-voice singing in the *Te Deum*, which— although it may seem heretical to admit—always seems to me a poor relation of the *Requiem*. Obviously Davis does not feel that way because as an interpretation this yields little or nothing to the larger work in conviction. Again there is the careful control of large forces, the comprehension of the two facets of Berlioz's conception—the majesty of God, the littleness of man—expressed in alternatingly awestruck and reverent music. The work, and interpretation, reach their climax in the final *Judex crederis*, its final section, as Cairns comments—and Davis makes us see—"swaying between splendour and terror like the swing of an enormous bell". The lovely pages of the *Te ergo quaesumus* are somewhat marred by the weak tenor soloist, but the final bars with the chorus singing the prayer, unaccompanied, *sotto voce*, are well brought off. I would not rate this one of the most successful of the Berlioz cycle, although there is little to fault in the conducting.

There need be no reservations whatsoever about the recording of *L'Enfance du Christ*. This Oiseau-Lyre recording was one of Colin's first essays into the studios—the set was made as long ago as October 1960, but it wears its years lightly. Davis has given many memorable performances of this work, which obviously, even in the context of his admiration of Berlioz's *oeuvres* as a whole, lies very close to his heart. As a general commendation I cannot improve on Alec Robertson's review of this recording back in 1961, when Davis's reputation as a Berliozian was itself in its infancy: "This performance of *L'Enfance du Christ* has all the qualities that I have for years dreamt of and longed for. Colin Davis evidently has an instinctive feeling for and understanding of Berlioz's music, and from start to finish there is not a suspicion of the 'oratorio style' in his conception of the exquisite work. He sees it as a true sacred drama—one indeed, that with an inspired producer might well be transferred to the stage and prove an immense success—devoid of theatricality. . . ."

Each movement deserves an encomium to itself. The depth of the string tone in the urgent introduction to Herod's aria has a typically Davis-like timbre, and the colouring of the wind and brass accompaniment to the aria itself produce that profound melancholy, that *mal d'isolment* from which the composer himself suffered. Joseph Rouleau as Herod sings here with wonderful richness and sympathy. Davis revels in the orchestration and quirky 7/4 rhythm of the Soothsayers' Chorus: those wind interpolations into the whirling, sinister strings come off brilliantly. Then the sudden upward string phrase, an evocation of Herod's terror, at "Que faut-il que je fasse?" as he sees his power threatened by the child Jesus could hardly be more arrestingly played than here.

As a complete contrast Davis captures the pure, peaceful lyricism of the

Mary and Joseph duet, a kind of sacred version of the still-unwritten *Troyens* love duet. The invisible angels are marvellously 'distanced' and the dying-away of the "Hosannas" at the end of this part is ravishing in this performance. The opening of "The Flight into Egypt" is again perfectly judged with relaxed, easy playing and singing from the Goldsborough Orchestra (now the ECO) and the St Anthony Singers. Peter Pears's simple singing of the Holy Family's Repose is echoed in the graceful 6/8 accompaniment from Davis and the orchestra. In the Journey to Saïs there is a sense of hopelessness and desperation as doors close behind the exhausted travellers. Once saved by the Ishmaelite family, they are succoured and entertained, and Davis provides the relaxation of this charming interlude. The final scene, with Pears unforgettable in his recitative, has the serenity and devoutness appropriate to a section described by Berlioz thus: "It seems to me to contain a feeling of infinite, of divine love". Davis may one day want to record this work again; he will find it hard to repeat the rightness and devotion of this reading.

Davis's two remaining Berlioz records, one from Philips, the other from Oiseau-Lyre, are a pleasing pendant to his recordings of the larger works; both consist of vocal pieces. They are certainly among my favourites in the series. The Philips recording of *Nuits d'Été* is given for the first time on disc as Berlioz intended, with the songs split between four singers and, although the continuity of one artist's interpretation is naturally missing, the gain in variety of timbre and correctness of keys is great. Davis's judging of speeds here seems just right. "Spectre de la Rose", for instance, is not dragged, "Sur les Lagunes" is given its proper weight, and "L'Ile inconnue" goes with a terrific swing. The singers, with the exception of the reedy tenor in his two offerings, could hardly be bettered. Veasey is radiant and eloquent in *Spectre de la Rose*, John Shirley-Quirk sombre and sad in "Sur les Lagunes", Sheila Armstrong sensitive and sensuous in the difficult "Absence", irresistible in "L'Ile inconnue".

The 'backing' is captivating. Here we have several much less well-known songs, all charmingly done. The gem, however, is Veasey's voluptuous account of *Captive*, where Davis provides an equally voluptuous support. Armstrong does almost as well by the skittish *Zaïde*, where Davis's lilting accompaniment plays a major part. For anyone who may not be quite the perfect Berliozian, these songs catch the essence of the composer's individual style—the long, irregular melodies, the haunting sense of a mood evoked by the peculiar timbre of his orchestration.

The Oiseau-Lyre disc is notable for *La Mort de Cléopatre*. From the wild, wilful introduction to the almost toneless final spasm of life as Cleopatra expires at the end, this early work—Berlioz's entry for the 1829 *Prix de Rome*—has exceptional power and originality, looking forward to so much in his later work. When criticised by his examiner Boieldieu, who found the harmonies incomprehensible, Berlioz commented that he found it difficult to write soothing music for an "Egyptian queen who has been bitten by a poisonous snake and is dying a painful death in an agony of remorse". Davis catches both the fury and frustration of the beginning and the typical Berlioz melody at "Ah! qu'ils sont loin ces jours", where Cleopatra recalls happier days. The "Méditation, Grands Pharaons", marked *sotto voce, con terrore* (throbbing strings, funereal brass)—a "rich, sombre effect", as the composer commented is inspiringly carried off, and

Studying at home—Kurosh looks on.

the fiercely dramatic outburst when the Queen declares that she will die by the bite of her "vil reptile" is a sheer *tour de force* as done here by Davis, Anne Pashley and the ECO. Those who may think this is an immature or disjointed work should hear what these artists make of it. It is, in many ways, a summing-up of Davis's complete identification with Berlioz that he can re-create this, one of the composer's most wonderful inspirations. There is nothing as exciting on the second side but *Sara la baigneuse* is a pleasing, flowing piece for mixed choir and in *La Mort d' Ophélie*, for a female chorus, Davis characterises what Hugh Macdonald in his sleeve-note so precisely calls its "refined delicacy and concentration of expression".

MOZART

There is a splendid consistency in Colin Davis's view of Mozart as represented on records from his first HMV disc, of *Eine kleine Nachtmusik*, through to his latest offerings. His is a very direct, unaffected approach that nonetheless does not exclude charm. As he said earlier, Mozart "rejoices in the gifts he was granted, and he puts them to the greatest possible use", and Colin is concerned only to give expression to those gifts without any kind of unnecessary embroidery. He shows his usual faithfulness to the written note and avoids eccentricities or exaggerations in his interpretations. Of late in the recording studio he seems to have been concentrating on the vocal works—operatic and sacred.

On his disc of the early A major and G minor Symphonies there is a balance and unaffected accentuation that suits these youthful masterpieces well. In both symphonies he makes the first-movement repeat, thus adding to the stature and formal proportions of the two works. Points of detail to note in the A major are the marvellous moment at the end of the slow movement when the mutes come off, the sheer *joie de vivre*, recalling Beecham in the same work, of the minuet and the high spirits of the finale. In the G minor, the clarity of the oboes and horns in the opening movement indicates Davis's insistence on keeping these pieces well in the eighteenth century (indeed in both works there is a feeling that these symphonies have emerged from a chamber music tradition, not from a concert-hall one). In the slow movement Davis's prime virtue of keeping a balance between classicism and romanticism in Mozart is very much to the fore. The finale has at once pace and control.

The later G minor Symphony is coupled with the E flat, No. 39. The opening movement of the G minor—again there is a repeat—is a real Allegro molto: this is a zippy, yet big-scale interpretation, a young man's reading—but what does that really mean? Certainly that it is lively, uncluttered by too much emotional weight, a touch impersonal?—perhaps. The slow movement is lucidly phrased, its development weighty, big-boned. The Minuet is as severe as the movement warrants with very marked staccato crotchets at the end of the first section. The finale is taken at an almost headlong pace with no mercy for the players until the second subject is reached. Here a sad smile comes over the music and the performance.

Rehearsing the chorus for the "Figaro" recording.

[*Phonogram*

Above: Countess (Jessye Norman) and conductor catch the mood of a scene at the "Figaro" recording sessions.

[Phonogram

Above right: Yvonne Minton (Cherubino) and Mirella Freni (Susanna).

[Phonogram

The introduction to the first movement of No 39 is Beethovenian, the Allegro very grand and dramatic—you often feel that Colin feels Mozart in terms of his operatic music. Davis requires his players to adopt really *piano* playing, both beautiful and exact, in the slow movement. The other two movements call for little comment because the interpretation seems always conceived along the right lines. This record is up among the best of these symphonies and of Davis's Mozart. The performances are very much ones to be lived with.

Davis's many concerto recordings are evidence enough of the value placed by soloists on his support. For him accompanying is not just another job. He takes very seriously the matter of working out an interpretation with a solo artist, and of course he likes to be in sympathy with their view of Mozart. I am certainly not going to offer individual comments on all these performances. I have favourites. The Sinfonia Concertante for violin and viola is one of these because of the sure rapport between Grumiaux, Pellicia, Davis and the LSO. This is a notoriously difficult work to bring off and old catalogues are strewn with many unsuccessful efforts. Here everything seems to fall into place: the balance is right, the phrasing of all concerned is unified, and above all the interpretation of the slow movement has that sad serenity and poised eloquence which lie at the core of one of the loveliest even among Mozart's slow movements. Davis sets exactly the right rocking tempo at the start and the playing reaches great heights of feeling without ever becoming in any way sentimental. The finale has the right sparkle and brio.

The violin concertos with Grumiaux are on the same level of achievement even if the music may not be quite so inspired. Malcolm Macdonald

Above: Scene from the recording session of Mozart's "Figaro".

[*Phonogram*

correctly characterised the accompaniment when he reviewed the disc of the B flat and the D major: "The orchestral playing does not limit its virtues to those of reticence when suitable, but also declares belief in phrasing and style, which are pointed in the highest degree". The same goes for Davis's conducting of the clarinet concerto with the impeccable Jack Brymer as soloist. There is excellent balance here, no skimping of the tuttis. Between them soloist and conductor have the speeds just right, not too slow or too fast, so that the Adagio flows and the finale sounds unflurried. The much less winning Flute and Harp Concerto on the reverse is a pleasing enough backing, and Davis ensures that the music keeps on the move.

The piano concertos with Ingrid Haebler in the mid-1960s were not all favourably received. Most of the adverse comments, however, referred to the solo playing rather than to Davis's accompanying. Musicianship and taste inform Haebler's playing, not often inspiration and insight. My favourite among the records she made with Colin (several of the series are with other conductors) is K450 and 451 which seem well suited to this pianist's style and reveal many of the excellent qualities of Davis's accompaniments: his attention to line, his ever-present rhythmic acuteness, and his fine balance between strings and wind. Listen to the beginning of K450's slow movement if you want to hear how much an expressive accompanist can matter.

Of the choral works, only Davis's record of the *Requiem* is at present available. In spite of a rather restricted range of choral sound as recorded—there is nothing wrong with the singing of the John Alldis Choir—this is the most recommendable version of the many available, simply because it is so intensely felt, so direct in expression—epithets that happily keep on

With Jessye Norman and producer Erik Smith at a playback of the "Figaro" recording

[Phonogram

coming to mind when dealing with his Mozart. There is a lack of affectation, an urgency about this performance that I have heard equalled but not surpassed by that other great Mozart conductor of our day, Britten. The deliberate, portentous tread of the *Rex tremendae*, the gentle consolation of *Recordare, pie Jesu*, the pathos of *Lacrimosa*, in fact every aspect of this ineffable work, is encompassed.

So far only *Idomeneo* and *Le Nozze di Figaro* of Colin's operatic interpretations are in the catalogue. *Idomeneo* has always meant something special to Colin. His revival at Sadler's Wells in 1962 did much to consolidate the good work already begun at Glyndebourne in the 1950s. His 1968 recording perpetuates his sound ideas on the opera. Stanley Sadie commented in *The Gramophone* when it was issued "The new recording captures splendidly the quality of excitement that pervades the score," and although he made several trenchant remarks about some of the casting—in particular the decision to have a tenor, rather than a soprano, Idamante —he ended by saying that "Its great strength is that it is a deeply committed performance under a conductor who obviously loves the work and believes in it passionately".

I wrote in *Opera*, and find on re-hearing no reason to change my opinion; "Throughout, Davis conducts with dramatic thrust, in the grand manner, bringing to this earlier piece the same sense of the theatre that Kleiber brought to *Figaro* and banishing once and for all the old, false assumption that this is a static or dusty opera. Above all, it is his handling of the accompanied recitative, in which the work abounds, that he—like Britten—brings the score to life. Perhaps he employs an orchestra sounding a little too large and unwieldy for the music but he draws from them, practically all of the time, precise, flexible playing. He has also imbued a polyglot cast, several of whom have probably not sung their parts on stage, with his own urgency and commitment."

There is no one definitive edition of *Idomeneo*. Before the first night Mozart, for various reasons, cut and cut again himself. Davis excludes Idamante's "No, la morte", included in the Glyndebourne recording, and most of Arbace's music. He includes "Torna la pace", sensibly excluded by Britten as it sits uncomfortably on the work's denouement, and mercifully does not snip bits out of arias in the bad, old Viennese way. In other words, this is more-or-less the version that Davis conducted at the Wells.

His singers have been carefully chosen. And I would like to point out here, in parentheses as it were, that Colin takes the greatest care over his cast in the sense that he will spend time helping to coach singers in their roles before a recording (I sat in one session for *Figaro* during which Colin was carefully going over Barbarina's little aria with a young singer specially chosen for the part: there was even an Italian coach present). That is why the sum of the parts in this recording is more satisfying than some of the individual singing. Still, there is nothing that mars the set, and George Shirley in the title role, Pauline Tinsley as Electra and Ryland Davies as the tenor Idamante are, for the most part, well inside their roles. Shirley, in particular, helped by strong support always makes the difficult coloratura of his arias meaningful.

Le Nozze di Figaro is another success. Davis's reading emphasises the serious dramatic side of the work—his account of the overture already tells us that—and there is little room for superficial charm in his reading.

In this vigorous interpretation, the clash of character and temperament are constantly to the fore. In musical terms this is expressed by bold phrasing, fastish tempos, and crisply articulated recitatives. Throughout the whole a dynamic pulse seems to throb, very much the pulse of teeming life.

The cast, in some respects unorthodoxly chosen, responds magnificently to Davis's lead. Ingvar Wixell's Count, strong, saturnine, arrogant, very much commands his household, and his singing is firm and pointed to match the vocal characterisation. His Countess, the young American soprano Jessye Norman, is no cipher beside him. Dignified and moving, she none the less conveys the inherent youthfulness of the young, poorly treated wife.

Wladimiro Ganzarolli is an ebullient, swaggering Figaro, occasionally a shade coarse vocally, but projecting the social consciousness of all the best interpreters. Mirella Freni, his Susanna, is able to suggest the character's quick wit and personal attraction by vocal means alone, and her singing is warm and fresh.

Yvonne Minton's Cherubino is a boyish, palpitating creation, although others have made more of "his" arias. The subsidiary roles are all well taken with Clifford Grant's powerful Bartolo—his aria is superbly sung—and Robert Tear's oily Basilio deserving special mention. The BBC Symphony Orchestra play with feeling, point and enjoyment. On the whole, the recording is worthy of the splendid performance.

Moment of tension as a point is checked with the control room.

[*Phonogram*

STRAVINSKY

Davis's Stravinsky may be rather more controversial than his Berlioz or Mozart simply because the composer's own performances are available on another label and must be regarded, of course, as authoritative versions, even when—as is sometimes the case—Davis may be even more faithful to the printed score. What is incontrovertible, however, is that Davis's continuing Stravinsky series with the LSO presents a level of technical accomplishment that would have been inconceivable only a few years ago.

Perhaps my favourite among the group is the disc that couples the Symphony in Three Movements with the ballet *Orpheus*. This neo-classical period of the composer seems to suit Davis's particular attributes very well. In the first movement there is the clarity of the texture to admire, an unfailing forte of all Davis's records, as I have come to realise. Perhaps this leads him to an almost too lithe view of this movement, which could do with a little more significance and weight (just the opposite qualities you find in Klemperer's reading), but I doubt if the textures and rhythms have ever been more pointed or inspiriting. The slow movement is a proper point of repose, lyrical and light. In the finale Davis's drive and athleticism come into their own, and he has a keen ear for its touches of humour, as when the fugal passage is cheekily begun by the piano and harp. *Orpheus* is impeccable with that feeling for other-worldliness, grave beauty and sadness for which the music is justly noted. The recording is among Philips's most spacious and clean.

The engineering again enhances the coupling of the Symphony in C and the ballet *Jeu de Cartes*. In the symphony Davis is particularly faithful

49

With Stephen Bishop at a playback of their Bartok/Stravinsky record.

[Phonogram

to the metronome and once more the interpretation has that hallmark of his Stravinsky, what Jeremy Noble called a combination of "rhythmic energy and lyrical elegance". I noticed the directness of the opening movement, the Mozartian grace of the slow movement, with the menacing note of the middle section given proper significance, and the delicacy of the Allegretto. Again, Davis's view of the composer seems very much influenced by him seeing the music through almost eighteenth-century eyes, or in his already-quoted words the restoration of sanity "after some of the excesses of the late nineteenth century". *Jeu de Cartes* displays again an even greater fidelity to the score than we find under the composer and other conductors. Without exaggeration, he manages to bring out the wit and coquetry of this likeable score.

And so to *The Rite of Spring*, which is a sort of Everest for conductors—it has to be conquered because it is there. Firstly, it must be said that in this case Philips did not succeed in doing full justice to the performance, and for that reason you will not find it on many people's list of first choice in this work. Which is a pity as the recording is not faulty enough to distract from the arresting account from Davis and the LSO. Again in a Davis performance it is the directness and honesty of approach that impresses: there is tremendous impetuosity in the "Mock Abduction", thrilling bravura attack in the "Adoration of the Earth". In many sections there are details that come up as if fresh-minted, emphasising the immediacy and originality of the work, as for instance when the muted strings tap out their broken triplet rhythm against a *pp* six-part chord sustained on flute and double bass harmonics in the introduction to the second part. "The Ritual of the Ancestors" is primitive as the composer always wanted it to be and the "Sacrificial Dance" is taut and brilliant, but not so fast as to lose precision. All in all, this vigorous, youthful interpretation can live with the best available, even with Boulez's and that is saying something.

Davis's remaining Stravinsky record for Philips is the Concerto for piano and wind, which is coupled with Bartók's Second Piano Concerto. Stephen Bishop is the soloist. This is an exciting pairing—both of artists and works. Bishop and Davis have often cooperated, and the partnership is so fruitful that one must hope they will make more records with each other. Here they relish the jazz elements in the Stravinsky and bring out its neo-classical outlines. Without ever relaxing their rhythmic control they suggest the inherent lyricism of the slow movement: it is tender without being sentimental. I would like a fairer balance in the Bartók where the piano is inclined to hog the microphone, but Bishop plays with such infectious strength and purpose that the balancing fault can almost be overlooked. The two gave this work at a 1966 Prom, and on other occasions, so it is not surprising to find their rapport so close or the feeling of spontaneity so vivid.

The record, in both senses, of Sadler's Wells's unforgettable production of *Oedipus Rex* has been long deleted by EMI: it should be restored forthwith. It is a match for the composer's version and keeps fresh the memory of the staging. Desmond Shawe-Taylor spoke of "its dramatic power and thrust" and went on to say that "he now naturally feels the theatrical force of passages which others (even Stravinsky himself) treat more as concert oratorio". That always happens, it seems to me, when a recording comes straight from a stage production. The playing of the

Royal Philharmonic sometimes leaves something to be desired, but the soloists and the fiery Sadler's Wells chorus of the day (1962–3) contribute boldly to the enterprise. Ronald Dowd's Oedipus is a rounded portrayal moving surely from the self-satisfied complacency of the beginning to the pathetic tragedy of the close and Patricia Johnson is a properly hard, driving Jocasta. Ralph Richardson's Narrator was much abused at the time the recording was issued; in retrospect I find his delivery unexceptional, not too declamatory nor too detached. But it is Davis's convincing and committed direction that really carries the day and imprints story and music ineradicably on the mind.

TIPPETT

We are very much in mid-stream where Davis's recordings of Tippett are concerned. The undoubted artistic and commercial success of *The Midsummer Marriage* may embolden Philips to record his other operas, indeed to commit themselves to a whole Tippett cycle. *The Midsummer Marriage* ranks among the most successful opera sets ever made, from every standpoint, and it forms an ideal introduction to the composer's music for the uninitiated. As we have seen Davis and Tippett seem to have an unspoken rapport with each other, or rather it is spoken about in one's interpretation of the other's music. As has been said Davis is to Tippett what Beecham was to Delius; for the moment Davis seems the person who can best unravel the complex skein of Tippett's words and music. Throughout, Davis has as John Warrack put it "the measure of this thronged, exhilarating, life-enhancing score". It is not a performance one wants to dissect any more than the seemingly dense text should be separated from the music. One should listen and be caught up in the work for oneself.

I would single out only two points for comment: the splendid majesty and depth of Tippett's and Davis's accompaniment to Sosostris's noble utterance, which is itself like a great Bach cantata aria in modern dress, and the marvellous final scene, where as throughout the recording Davis commands his large forces with consummate ease and, with the help of the very spacious and atmospheric recording (for which we must thank Erik Smith), the piece comes to life before us. Indeed imagining the action in our minds enables us to understand the meaning of it much more closely than either of the productions so far seen, both of which were too earthbound and heavy for this ethereal score. The cast, headed by Joan Carlyle's full-blooded, purely sung Jennifer, Raimund Herincx's bold King Fisher and Helen Watts's impressive Sosostris is uniformly good.

The Second Symphony, recorded by Argo, has the same sort of qualities as Davis's Stravinsky, above all vitality, clarity and confidence. The Stravinsky analogy spills over into the music as far as the first movement is concerned. The opening shows the vigour and energy of performance and music giving way to what Robert Layton called the "intoxicating lyrical atmosphere of the second group". The second movement has in this recording the mystery and otherworldliness Davis himself speaks about as being part and parcel of Tippett. Luminous is the only word to describe the textures hereabouts. The challenge of the rhyth-

"Conducting" at a playback of "The Midsummer Marriage" recording.

[Michael H. Evans

Elizabeth Harwood as Bella, Stuart Burrows as Jack in "The Midsummer Marriage" at Covent Garden.

[Phonogram

mically exploratory scherzo, with its heavy long beats against light short ones, is met and conquered in this performance. I remember just how thrilling this and the brilliant finale were in a Festival Hall performance with the LSO. Once again Davis shows how he can repeat that kind of tension in the studio. He seems to be able to forget himself in the music and forget the myriad technical problems, which unlike some conductors he leaves to those who specialise in overcoming them to work out. Incidentally, the recorded sound here is superbly vivid.

So is it on Davis's recording of Tippett's *Concerto for Orchestra*, one of his most haunting works. It was commissioned for the 1963 Edinburgh Festival when Davis and the LSO gave the first performance. The fascinating contrasts of colour in the first movement, the intense, rather complex Lento for strings, harp and piano, and the panache of the finale, where the whole orchestra comes together for the first time in the work, are all conveyed in the brilliance of performance and recording. Whereas the Concerto for Orchestra inhabits the world of *King Priam*, the Piano Concerto (both discs came out in the month of the composer's sixtieth birthday, March 1965), is in the same vein as *The Midsummer Marriage*. Davis understands and enjoys one idiom as much as the other.

BEETHOVEN
and others

One day Colin will doubtless have the opportunity of recording *Fidelio*. At present his Beethoven is represented in the catalogue only by three of the symphonies and some overtures. The symphonies were recorded in the reverse order of their composition. Indeed the Seventh was one of his earliest discs and it remains among his best. His measured pace for this work's opening movement helps the clarity and tension here. The slow movement is very fine with a truly *pianissimo* start and a marvellous swell of sound to *ff* and back. The string counterpoint, when the wind have the theme, is beautifully clear and the fugato is judged well to fit in with the basic tempo of the movement. The scherzo is very brisk; the trio much slower in comparison. The finale is fast and vigorous but never a scramble: the repeats in this movement add enormously to its stature. For an interpretation that is straightforward and without eccentricities this one is hard to beat. There is not too much luxuriating in sound for its own sake, plenty of attention to structure and the relationship of tempi. I notice this in the other two symphonies too, although all three have been recorded at fairly wide intervals. Excellent EMI sound.

The *Pastoral* for Philips, coupled with an exhilarating account of the *Prometheus* overture, is another attractive reading. As his Mozart is sometimes Beethovenian, so paradoxically Davis's Beethoven is here rather Mozartian. The opening Allegro is kept on the move with a fairly rhythmic bounce and precise attention to the staccato markings. The second movement is very classical, not so much a walk through the countryside as some idealised, more abstract view; Claude is suggested, perhaps, as in the *Symphonie Fantastique*. The scherzo is again airy and light with Davis's familiar attention to the *pianissimo* markings. The storm seems here like a partner of the *Don Giovanni* finale, very dramatic, not too deliberately picturesque; indeed the onomatopoeia is somewhat played down. The last movement is again purposeful and Mozartian with hardly a peep into the nineteenth century.

The more recent *Eroica* has the BBC Symphony instead of the usual LSO and there is some loss in the quality of the string playing, though none in winds and brass. There is an advantage, however, in having an orchestra that has done this work quite often with Davis over the past few years: there is no doubting their complete comprehension of his reading. He seems anxious, also in this work, to avoid trying to look back at this symphony through over-romantic eyes; the interpretation is 'absolute' and uncluttered. That is not to say it lacks emotional content: the Funeral March is built up to an almost overwhelming climax and sinks away in exhaustion. Davis's involvement here is expressed physically by the odd audible groan. In the opening movement Davis employs a wide dynamic range and reminds us in Boulez's comment in another context to "stretch our ears" as the first listeners certainly must have done: in other words those stark chords are punched out almost fiercely.

I also noticed something in these first two movements that had not struck me before: how the texture of this symphony is similar to that of *Fidelio*, written about the same time. The scherzo is taken at a just pace, not as slow as Klemperer or as quick as Toscanini; just right, in fact. The variations of the finale move inevitably one into the other, and the noble slow one is grandly conceived. I think this interpretation has been caught at just the right time, and has added to Davis's stature as a classicist. He has conducted the Ninth several times over the past two or three years, but he will probably wait a few years until he commits that to disc. Perhaps we can expect some of the other even-numbered symphonies before long. The fill-up to the *Eroica* is a powerful *Coriolan Overture*. The Philips recording on this disc, spacious and alert, is a great improvement on that for the Sixth.

The Bishop–Davis combination has already made two excellent records of the Beethoven piano concertos—the first in C and the *Emperor*. In both the rapport is again notable, Bishop's clear, direct playing being complemented by Davis's unfussy accompanying. Both artists, putting Beethoven first, avoid eccentricities of interpretation; both readings are deeply considered with Davis a model accompanist, seconding his soloist promptly, launching each movement with a firm, well-chosen speed, which is then maintained throughout with the minimum of changes. (The partnership has been renewed in a record coupling the Schumann and Grieg concertos.)

Davis has not been very much associated with the late nineteenth-century repertory, and so some may be surprised to find just how successful is his record of the Dvorák *Symphonic Variations*. This quite unjustifiably neglected score is here given a clearly moulded and loving interpretation, most warmly recorded. Davis observes the symphonic character of the composition—it is not very symphonic in construction—and yet finds time to linger in some of Dvorák's more eloquent moments. The more dance-like variations are ebullient and carefree. The other side contains a disarmingly fresh account of the more popular *Serenade*.

Mid-session conference with Heather Harper while recording "Messiah".

[Phonogram

All passion—and time—spent.
Colin Davis discusses the session
with Erik Smith of Phonogram.

[Phonogram

A much, much earlier disc, made for World Record Club, and now on Classics for Pleasure, has an equally attractive account of the Brahms *St Antoni Variations*—no lack of sympathy here for a composer whose works he is supposed to be reluctant to conduct. The rest of this disc is more variable: a dramatic rendering of the *Fidelio* overture, a rather lacklustre *Hebrides*, and an unremarkable *Siegfried Idyll*. The recording and playing (Sinfonia of London) is none too vivid. A much more recent Philips disc includes a more successful *Hebrides* plus excellent accounts of, among others, the *Meistersinger* and *Freischütz* overtures.

Davis has not yet been associated very closely with Elgar. One wonders why after hearing his record of the *Enigma Variations* coupled with the *Cockaigne* overture. Trevor Harvey put it as well as I ever could when he said that "Elgar himself, I think, would have been delighted and, so no doubt, will Elgarians at large. It is basically traditional, but each variation is, at the same time, seen with a fresh and most perceptive eye". That is a view confirmed by concert performances I have heard from Davis of this work. To quote Harvey again: "Detail is acutely observed and beautifully expressed: there is not a point in Elgar's scoring that goes for nothing. This is not just another record of a much-recorded work. I ended by thinking what a masterpiece it all is . . ." *Cockaigne* pleased him, and me, less. Here for once Davis seems just to miss the spirit of a piece. Perhaps he deliberately played down the Edwardian opulence and swagger in the music; in consequence the music sounds a little apologetic. As always, Davis draws exciting performances from the LSO.

Colin has explained his equivocal attitude to Elgar thus: "My father

loved the music of Elgar and I listened to records of the *Introduction and Allegro* and the *Nursery Suite* as a very small boy, listened unspoilt by ideas I was too young to have come across. By the time I was fifteen and fanatical about music I excluded Elgar from my narrow range of heroes, although I was still hearing scraps of his music, particularly the theme from the A flat Symphony and parts of the *Enigma Variations*, which I remember were often played as voluntary in our school chapel. I was also one of a party that travelled to London to hear *The Dream of Gerontius*, an expedition organised out of kindness by the same organist who played for the school services—but I didn't like the work. It was not at all in tune with my intolerant enthusiasms.

"Then in the early 1960s, at the instigation of the LSO, I learned the First Symphony, reluctantly to begin with, but with increasing respect. Here was a remarkable composer of prodigious vitality, warmth and sensitivity. Grand certainly, but no more absurd in his grandeur than Gibbon in his symphonic prose. I liked it, and would like to think it were possible that I hear Elgar's music now as I did when I was five years old, before heart and brain were confused by the world."

There remain to discuss Purcell's *Dido and Aeneas*, two choral recordings —*Messiah* and *The Seasons*—and various odds and ends. The *Messiah* is perhaps the most important of these sets because it was the first performance taking account of eighteenth-century practice in style of performance (just pipping Charles Mackerras and EMI to the post). The booklet tells us that Davis worked out stylistically appropriate embellishments for each individual singer. The orchestra consists of 31 strings, two

oboes, two bassoons, two trumpets, timpani, chamber organ, and harpsichord. The chorus has 40 voices. The recording, goes the note, "also seeks to escape from the oppressive weightiness and sombre atmosphere, which became typical in the nineteenth century". This is partly achieved by, in places, double-dotting, particularly in the overture "where the conductor feels it is called for from the point of view of musical effect and eighteenth-century practice".

The intentions have been carried out with complete thoroughness: there is no trace of the sentimental aura that used to surround this work. Textures are light, rhythms crisp and even bouncing, speeds are on the fast side. Desmond Shawe-Taylor wrote that it was "by far the most enjoyable performance I can recall. The delightfully brisk allegro choruses are as clear as daylight, and the more solemn ones lose nothing in grandeur. 'For unto us' renews all our wonder at the sublime invention of this merry homage to the incarnate deity; and 'Surely He hath borne' is 'one of the many sorrowful numbers which show how deeply Mr Davis has delved into this score."

I had certain reservations when the set first appeared: it seemed to me then that everything was perhaps too relentlessly lively. On returning to the performance I found my former doubts almost all swept away in the sheer sense of vigour and enjoyment. My notes are covered with approval for the spontaneity of choruses such as "He shall purify" where the LSO Chorus articulate their semiquavers to perfection, and for the buoyancy and elasticity of "All we like sheep". Even "Let us break", so difficult to bring off, is here accurate and meaningful. In the "Hallelujah", there is no trace of the usual portentousness.

The soloists are well attuned to Davis's reading. Heather Harper manages to keep up with the very fast speed set for "Rejoice greatly", and is eloquence itself in "I know that my Redeemer". Her little embellishments in "Come unto him" are very attractive. Helen Watts is the most expressive alto. With Davis she has worked out sensible ornamentation for "He was despised", and is absolutely on the dot in the middle section. John Wakefield is the committed if not very mellifluous tenor: how his recitatives beginning "Thy rebuke" are enhanced by the appropriate appoggiaturas. These, too, are not sentimentalised and are all the more moving for that. John Shirley-Quirk is not your rollicking bass soloist of tradition, but his sensitive and varied tone is much preferable to any blustering. I particularly appreciated the controlled vigour he and Davis bring to "Why do the Nations". The LSO play marvellously, and the Philips recording is well balanced. There is strong competition from the Mackerras set. I would not be without either.

Davis has always been an enthusiastic advocate of *The Seasons*, and his recorded performance brings out all the dramatic flair and warm affection of his concert performances. He uses the English text, and so his version is in a sense complementary to Böhm's recording on DGG, a suaver, more sophisticated reading. Davis is at once vigorous and delicate. Earthy ebullience courses through the choruses, especially that inspiring one that describes the hunt, while those hushed moments when Haydn stands in awe of nature—at the lowering clouds of summer in Part 2 or in the wonderful C minor evocation of winter's approach in the introduction to Part 4—are given real presence. "Winter" is, in many ways, the most forward-looking music Haydn wrote—the Schubertian F major aria for Lucas, the noble, romantic breadth of Simon's musings on earth's transitoriness—and this aspect is fully realised by Davis, who is adept at characterising the mood of each part.

He worked wonders with the BBC Chorus and Symphony Orchestra, at least after a somewhat stodgy "Spring", and the Philips engineers achieved a spacious recording, although the volume control needs to be turned up to get good results. The soloists, who are a kind of Davis team, contribute strongly to the success of this venture. Harper sings very clearly, surely, and with a nice touch of humour (in relating the tale of the "honest country lass" outwitting a lord). Ryland Davis matches his firm, lyric tenor neatly to the text as does John Shirley-Quirk, although some of the music lies a little low for him. Maurits Sillem adds much telling detail on the fortepiano in the recitatives.

Davis takes a briskly dramatic view of *Dido and Aeneas*, a neatly complementary set to his *Les Troyens* with Veasey again as the heroine. His view is as far away as could be imagined from mere reverence for a historical document; he rightly treats the work as being as valid today as it

Below left: Gillian Knight—a most un-witch-like Witch in the recording of "Dido and Aeneas".

[Phonogram

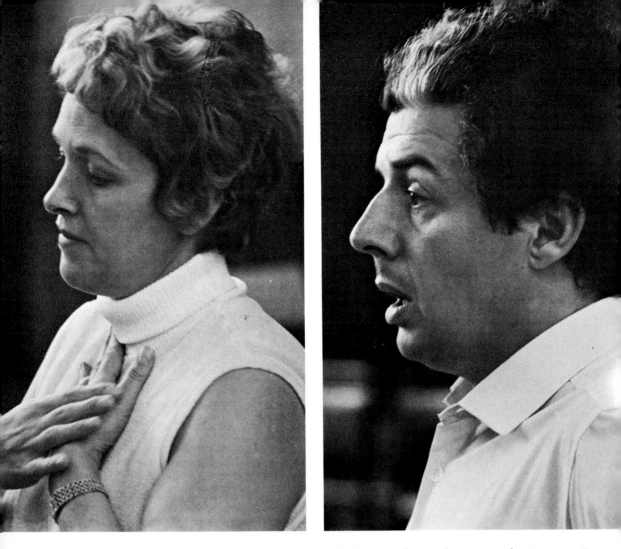

Above: Josephine Veasey and John Shirley-Quirk as Dido and Aeneas in the recording of Purcell's opera.

[*Phonogram*

was 300 years ago. Again there is a flow and purpose in his interpretation. However, I wish he had not allowed John Constable (who is the version's editor) so much leeway at the harpsichord: his part is too ornate and, as recorded, too prominent. In a performance of Purcell's work, you do not want to be constantly aware of the continuo. On the other hand, the Academy of St Martin's are not balanced closely enough to let us hear their fine work clearly. Veasey is a grandly passionate heroine, greatly aided by a close rapport with Davis. Shirley-Quirk is no less impressive as Aeneas: his final recitative is deeply affecting. Helen Donath is a lively, urgent Belinda whose exemplary diction is up to the standard set by the two principals. All the smaller parts are well cast.

There are several other excellent versions—the work is nearly as often recorded as *Tosca*—and I would hesitate to declare Davis's an outright winner. A work as great as this one is open to many interpretations, equally valid, but his is among the most enjoyable.

An even more desirable record (sadly now unavailable) from ten years earlier, contains five Rossini overtures. For those who may think that Davis is primarily a serious conductor unable to unbend in lesser or at least lighter music should correct the impression by trying to own or at least hear this disc. Indeed, the way he handles these overtures is proof enough why Colin's career suddenly took wing—as these pieces take wing. He had a Royal Philharmonic whose memory of Beecham was still very fresh and the performances have a Beechamesque flick-of-the-wrist to them that is utterly disarming. In *Gazza Ladra* one can almost see Colin swinging into the main tune, and throughout the wind playing has a tripping delicacy to it, and the strings are alert and fizzing. *Semiramide* has the same sort of precision, and the famous crescendo in *William Tell* is tremendous both times round. EMI should surely reissue this disc on its Classics for Pleasure label.

His recording of Wagner excerpts, including two very rare items, with Birgit Nilsson, proves beyond doubt Colin's sympathy with this composer, particularly in the Wesendonck songs. Here, too, Nilsson sings with her usual eloquence and also with great delicacy.

Two other operatic discs of about the same vintage are less winning. The Sadler's Wells *Carmen* excerpts find Davis unaccustomedly careful and retiring. Perhaps the "Highlight" format did not let him really shape the performance. I seem to remember it had more "go" in the opera house. That record dates from 1961. The disc of arias with Anna Moffo, made as long ago as 1959, is more successful, at least on Davis's part. He shows himself sympathetic to Donizetti and Bellini—and to the singer, who is not quite in her best voice. The record is available nowadays on a Regal-EMI import.

Still earlier in 1959—in fact one of Colin's first records—came Mozart's "Night Music". It must be popular, and deservedly so, as it is still in the catalogue. The orchestra sounds a little on the large size for works like *Eine kleine Nachtmusik* and the *Serenata Notturna*, but the playing is so sensitively phrased and stylish that you only notice any heaviness in the tuttis.

This is very much an interim report on Davis and his recording career. So much remains for him to tackle, but sensibly he wants to have stage and concert experience of works before he commits them to disc. One day we shall have a B minor Mass, a *Fidelio*, a *Missa Solemnis*, perhaps an *Otello*, *Ring* and *Tristan* from him. These will doubtless be as immediate, as personal, as honest as his Berlioz, Mozart, Stravinsky and Tippett. Routine is the one thing that is anathema to Colin. Everything must be fresh and spontaneous; everything must fit into the philosophy, the way of running his life, that he has worked out for himself, so much helped by his second wife Shamsi, whom he married in 1964. They and their two sons live simply and happily in Highbury, where music, for all its importance in Colin's life, is not allowed to spill over or spoil personal relationships. None the less Colin is certain of one thing: that his music-making must be related to the world around him and to our reasons for being in that world.

❦ Colin Davis ❦

A Discography

Record categories

Index Letters	Numbers	Example	Type of Record
Roman Capitals	Roman	T43	Mono LP
Bold Face Capitals	Bold	**ST43**	Stereo LP
Italic lower case	Italic	*7p361*	Mono SP
Italic Capitals	Italic	*SEL1692*	Mono EP
Bold Face lower case	Bold Face	**esl6294**	Stereo EP
Reversed out	Bold Face	4	Tape cassette
		8	Tape cartridge

(T) denotes 3¾ i.p.s. mono reel-to-reel tape

Abbreviated Names of Orchestras

BBC SO	BBC Symphony Orchestra	New SO	New Symphony Orchestra of London
ECO	English Chamber Orchestra	Philh.	Philharmonia Orchestra
LPO	London Philharmonic Orchestra	RPO	Royal Philharmonic Orchestra
LSO	London Symphony Orchestra	SoL	Sinfonia of London

Notes
All records issued by Philips Records unless otherwise marked

A.	Angel (USA)	Cap	Capitol (USA)	RCA	RCA (UK)
Am. Wing	Wing (USA)	D	Decca (UK)	O-L	Oiseau-Lyre (UK)
Am. P.	Philips (USA)	H	His Master's Voice (UK)	Sera	Seraphim (USA)
Am. RCA	RCA (USA)	MFP	Music for Pleasure (UK)	WRC	World Record Club (UK)
C	Columbia (UK)	R	Regal (UK: Export only)		

1958 Mozart. Symphonies: No. 29 in A major, K201; No. 39 in E flat major, K543
SoL
WRC T43/**ST43**
WRC (T) TT43
Am. RCA**VICS1378**
MFP **CFP102**

1958 Mozart. Symphony No. 34 in C major, K338
Oboe Concerto in C major, K314★
SoL ★with Leon Goossens (oboe)
WRC T59/**ST59**
WRC (T) TT59
Am. RCA**VICS1382**

1958 "COLIN DAVIS CONDUCTS"
Brahms. Variations on a theme of Haydn, Op. 56a, "St. Antoni"
Beethoven. Fidelio—Overture, Op. 72
Mendelssohn. Hebrides Overture, Op. 26, "Fingal's Cave"
Wagner. Siegfried Idyll
SoL
WRC T60/**ST60**
WRC (T) TT60
MFP **CFP140**

1959 May Mozart. Serenade No. 13 in G major, K525, "Eine kleine Nachtmusik"
Three German Dances, K605
Minuet in C major, K409
Divertimento No. 17 in D major, K334: Minuet
Serenade No. 6 in D major, K239, "Serenata Notturna"
Philh.
H. XLP20019/**SXLP20019**
Sera. **S–60057**

1959 December "OPERATIC ARIAS"—ANNA MOFFO (soprano)
Donizetti. LUCIA DI LAMMERMOOR: Il dolce suono . . . Ardon gl' incensi
Rossini. IL BARBIERE DI SIVIGLIA: Una voce poco fà
Bellini. I PURITANI: Qui la voce★
Bellini. LA SONNAMBULA: Ah! non credea mirarti . . . Ah! non giunge★
Verdi. RIGOLETTO: Gualtier Maldè . . . Caro nome†
Verdi. LA TRAVIATA: E strano! . . . Ah! fors' è lui . . . Sempre libera†
Philh.
C. 33CX1728/**SAX2376**
A. 35861/**S35861**
R. **SREG2064**

Items marked ★ also on C. SEL1692/**esl6294**
Items marked † also on C. SEL1698/**esl6297**

1959 Rachmaninov. Piano Concerto No. 2 in C minor, Op. 18 with Peter Katin (piano), New SO
D ACL237

1960 March Mozart. Divertimenti: No. 10 in F major, K247; No. 11 in D major, K251
ECO   O-L OL50198/**SOL60029**

1960 September and **October** Mozart. Concertone in C major for two violins, oboe, cello and orchestra, K190 Haydn. Symphony No. 84 in E flat major
ECO   O-L OL50199/**SOL60030**

1960 October Berlioz. L'ENFANCE DU CHRIST—complete with Elsie Morison, Peter Pears, Edgar Fleet, John Cameron, Joseph Rouleau, John Frost, St. Anthony Singers, Goldsbrough Orchestra
O-L OL50201–2/**SOL60032–3**

1961 February Mozart. Overtures: Così fan tutte★; The Impresario; The Abduction from the Seraglio; Magic Flute; Don Giovanni; Idomeneo; Clemenza di Tito; Finta Giardiniera; Marriage of Figaro★
RPO   H. CLP1506/**CSD1406**
             WRC T691/**ST691**
             WRC (T) TT691
             Sera. **S-60037**
Items marked ★ also on   H. 7p297

1961 April Beethoven. Symphony No. 7 in A major, Op. 92
RPO   H. XLP20038/**SXLP20038**

1961 April, June and **October** Rossini. Overtures: William Tell; Thieving Magpie★; Semiramide; Signor Bruschino; Italian Girl in Algiers
RPO   H. CLP1556/**CSD1436**
Item marked ★ also on   H. 7p361

1961 June Stravinsky. Danses concertantes; Concerto in E flat major, "Dumbarton Oaks"; Concerto in D major for strings
ECO   O-L OL50219/**SOL60050**

1961 June Mozart. Symphonies: No. 33 in B flat major, K319; No. 36 in C major, K425, "Linz"
ECO   O-L OL50218/**SOL60049**

1961 June J. C. Bach. Symphonies, Op. 18: No. 1 in E flat major; No. 3 in D major; No. 4 in D major
ECO   O-L **SOL317**

1961 June Weber. Clarinet Concerto No. 2 in E flat major, Op. 74 Spohr. Clarinet Concerto No. 1 in C minor, Op. 26 with Gervase de Peyer (clarinet), LSO (section)   O-L OL50214/**SOL60035**

1961 October Bizet. CARMEN—excerpts (in English) with Patricia Johnson, Elizabeth Robson, Donald Smith, Raimund Herincx, Sadler's Wells Chorus and
Orchestra   H. CLP1493/**CSD1398**
                   Cap P8605/**SP8605**

1961 November Mozart. Violin Concertos: No. 3 in G major, K216; No. 5 in A major, K219

with Arthur Grumiaux (violin), LSO
A02224L/**835112AY**
Am. P. 4 **18127CAA**

1961 November Mozart. Symphonies: No. 39 in E flat major, K543; No. 40 in G minor, K550
LSO   A02225L/**835113AY**
             6580 029

1961 November Stravinsky. OEDIPUS REX—complete with Patricia Johnson, Sir Ralph Richardson, Ronald Dowd, Raimund Herincx, Sadler's Wells Chorus, RPO
H. ALP1960/**ASD511**
A. 35778/**S35778**

1961 December Mozart. Piano Concertos: No. 19 in F major, K459; No. 26 in D major, K537 with Ingrid Haebler (piano), LSO
6717 001
SAL3753

1962 March and **April; 1966 September** Berlioz. La Mort de Cleopatre★
Sara la Baigneuse, Op. 11†
Meditation Religieuse, Op. 18 No. 1†
La Mort d'Ophelie, Op. 18 No. 2† ECO
Item marked ★ with Anne Pashley; † with St. Anthony Singers   O-L OL304/**SOL304**

1962 April Berlioz. BEATRICE ET BENEDICT—complete with Josephine Veasey, April Cantelo, Helen Watts, John Mitchinson, John Shirley-Quirk, Eric Shilling, St. Anthony Singers, LSO
O-L OL256–7/**SOL256–7**

1962 April Mozart. Violin Concertos: No. 1 in B flat major, K207; No. 4 in D major, K218 with Arthur Grumiaux (violin), LSO
AL3440/**SAL3440**
Am. P. **835 136**
Am. P. 4 **18142CAA**

1962 April Beethoven. Symphony no. 6 in F major, Op. 68, "Pastoral"; Creatures of Prometheus, Op. 43—
Overture   A02251L/**835133AY**
LSO   4 **CPC0016**
             Am. P. 4 **18112CAA**
Beethoven. Leonore Overture No. 2, Op. 72
LSO   unissued

1962 July Stravinsky. Cantata on old English texts; Mass with Doreen Murray, Jean Allister, Patricia Kern, Alexander Young, Edgar Fleet, Christopher Keyte, ECO
O-L OL265/**SOL265**

1962 October Berlioz. Harold in Italy, Op. 16 with Yehudi Menuhin (viola), Philh.
H. ALP1986/**ASD537**
A. 36123/**S36123**

1962 Grieg. Piano Concerto in A minor, Op. 16 Litolff. Concerto Symphonique, Op. 102—Scherzo with Peter Katin (piano), LPO
D **SPA170**

1962 December Mozart. Symphonies: No. 28 in C major, K200; No. 38 in D major, K504, "Prague"
ECO   O-L OL266/**SOL266**

1963 May Berlioz. Symphonie fantastique, Op. 14
LSO   AL3441/**SAL3441**
        Am. P. **835 188**
        Am. P. 4 **PCR4–900–101**
        Am. P. 8 **PC8–900–101**

1963 November Stravinsky. The Rite of Spring
LSO   AL3471/**SAL3471**
        Am. P. **6580 013**
        (cassette: 18180CAA)

1963 November Mozart. Symphonies: No. 25 in G minor, K183★; No. 29 in A major, K201†; No. 32 in G major, K318
LSO   AL3502/**SAL3502**
        Am. P. **835 262**
Item marked ★ also on   P. 4 **CPC0071**
Item marked † also on   P. 4 **CPC0041**

1963 December Tippett. Piano Concerto.
with John Ogdon (piano), Philh.
        H. ALP2073/**ASD621**

1963 December, 1964 January Mozart. Flute Concertos: No. 1 in G major, K313; No. 2 in D major, K314
Andante in C major for flute and orchestra, K315
Hubert Barwahser (flute), LSO
        AL3499/**SAL3499**
Item marked ★ also on   4 **CPC0041**
Item marked † also on   4 **CPC0071**

1964 January Mozart. Flute and Harp Concerto in C major, K299
Hubert Barwahser (flute), Osian Ellis (harp), LSO
        AL3535/**SAL3535**
        4 **CPC0012**

1964 January Stravinsky. Orpheus
Symphony in three movements
LSO   AL3490/**SAL3490**

1964 May Mozart. Sinfonia Concertante in E flat major, K364★
Violin Concerto No. 2 in D major, K211
Arthur Grumiaux (violin), LSO
Item marked ★ also with Arrigo Pellicia (viola)
        AL3492/**SAL3492**
        Am. P. **835 256**
Mozart. Rondo in C major for violin and orchestra, K373
Adagio in E major for violin and orchestra, K261
Arthur Grumiaux (violin), LSO unissued

Mozart. Clarinet Concerto in A major, K622
Jack Brymer (clarinet), LSO
        AL3535/**SAL3535**
        4 **CPC0012**
Mozart. Symphony No. 14 in A major, K114
LSO   **CXL25**

1964 August Tippett. Concerto for Orchestra
LSO   AL3497/**SAL3497**

1964 September Mozart. Piano Concertos: No. 15 in B flat major, K450★; No. 16 in D major, K451
Ingrid Haebler (piano), LSO
        AL3545/**SAL3545**
        AXS12000
Item marked ★ also on   6717 001

1964 Rodrigo. Concierto de Aranjuez
with Julian Bream (guitar), Melos Chamber Orchestra
        Am. RCA LM2730/**LSC2730**
        RCA RB6635/**SB6635**

1965 January Elgar. Variations on an original theme, Op. 36, "Enigma"
Cockaigne Overture, Op. 40
LSO   AL3516/**SAL3516**
        4 **CPC0024**
        Am. P. **835 317**
        Am. P. 4 **18123CAA**

1965 May Mozart. Piano Concertos: No. 24 in C minor, K491; No. 14 in E flat major, K449★
Ingrid Haebler (piano), LSO
        SAL3642
        AXS12000
Item marked ★ also on   6717 001

1965 September Stravinsky. Symphony in C; Jeu de Cartes★
LSO   AL3572/**SAL3572**
Item marked ★ also on   Am. P. 4 **18176CAA**

1965 September Tchaikovsky. Piano Concerto No. 2 in G major, Op. 44
with Nikita Magaloff (piano), LSO
        SGL5873
Weber. Konzertstück in F minor for piano and orchestra, J282
with Nikita Magaloff (piano), LSO
        unissued

1965 October Mozart. Piano Concertos: No. 13 in C major, K415★; No. 11 in F major, K413
Ingrid Haebler (piano), LSO
        SAL3645
        AXS12000
Item marked ★ also on   6717 001
        4 **CPC0022**
Berlioz. Overtures: King Lear, Op. 4; Les Francs Juges, Op. 3; Roman Carnival, Op. 9; Waverley, Op. 2b; Corsair, Op. 21
LSO   AL3573/**SAL3573**
        Am. P. **835 367**
        4 7300 080

1966 June and **July** Handel. MESSIAH—complete
with Heather Harper, Helen Watts, John Wakefield, John Shirley-Quirk, LSO Choir, LSO
        AL3584–6/**SAL3584–6**
        6703 001
        Am. P. **SC 71 AX 300**

Excerpts from complete recording
SAL3623
4 CPC0005
Am.P. 4 PCR4–900–214
Am.P. 8 PC8–900–214

1966 September Mozart. Piano Concertos: No. 18 in
B flat major, K456; No. 22 in E flat major, K482
Ingrid Haebler (piano), LSO
AXS12000
SAL3740
6717 001

1967 March Tippett. Symphony No. 2
LSO   Argo ZRG535

1968 February and March Berlioz. Roméo et Juliette,
Op. 17
with Patricia Kern, Robert Tear, John Shirley-Quirk,
John Alldis Choir, LSO
SAL3695–6
6700 032
Am. P. 839 716/17

1967 September Mozart. Requiem Mass in D minor,
K626
with Helen Donath, Yvonne Minton, Ryland Davis,
Gerd Nienstedt, John Alldis Choir, BBC SO
SAL3649
4 CPC0025
Am. P. 4 PCR4–900–160
Am. P. 8 PC8–900–160
Am. P. 802 862

1968 February and March Dvořák. Symphonic
Variations, Op. 78; Serenade in E major, Op. 22
LSO   SAL3706
Am. P. 839 706

1968 June and July Haydn. THE SEASONS—complete
with Heather Harper, Ryland Davies, John Shirley-
Quirk, BBC Chorus, BBC SO
SAL3747–9
6703 023
Am. P. 839 719/21

1968 September Mozart. IDOMENEO—complete
with Margherita Rinaldi, Pauline Tinsley, George
Shirley, Ryland Davies, Robert Tear, Donald Pilley,
Stafford Dean, BBC Chorus, BBC SO
SAL3747–9
6703 024
Am. P. 839 758/60

1968 December Bartók. Piano Concerto No. 2
with Stephen Bishop (piano), BBC SO
SAL3779
Am. P. 839761
4 7300 003

1969 January Berlioz. Te Deum, Op. 22
with Franco Tagliavini, Wandsworth School Boys'
Choir, LSO Chorus, LSO
SAL3724
Am. P. 839790
4 CPC0083
Am. P. 4 18244CAA

1969 April Stravinsky. Concerto for piano and wind
instruments
with Stephen Bishop (piano), BBC SO
SAL3779
Am. P. 839761
4 7300 003

1969 May Beethoven. Piano Concerto No. 5 in E flat
major, Op. 73, "Emperor"
with Stephen Bishop (piano), LSO
SAL3787
Am. P. 839794
4 7300 010

1969 May and June Berlioz. Prelude, The Trojans at
Carthage
Symphonie funèbre et triomphale, Op. 15★
Marche funèbre, Op. 18 No. 3 (for the last act of
"Hamlet")
LSO. Item marked ★ with John Alldis Choir
SAL3788
Am. P. 802913
4 7300 021

1969 June Berlioz. Les nuits d'été, Op. 7
La belle voyageuse, Op. 2 No. 4
La chasseur danois, Op. 19 No. 6
La captive, Op. 12
Le jeune patre breton, Op. 13 No. 4
Zaide, Op. 19 No. 1
with Sheila Armstrong, Josephine Veasey, Frank
Patterson, John Shirley-Quirk, LSO
6500 009
4 7300 015

1969 September "THE LAST NIGHT OF THE
PROMS"
Live recording made in the Royal Albert Hall
on Saturday September 13th
Elgar. Cockaigne Overture, Op. 40; Pomp and
Circumstance March No. 1 in D major, Op. 39
Wood. Fantasia on British Sea Songs
Parry (arr Elgar). Jerusalem
Speech by Colin Davis at the conclusion of the concert
BBC SO   SFM23033
6502 001
4 7304 002

1969 September and October Berlioz. LES TROYENS
—complete
with Jon Vickers, Josephine Veasey, Berit Lindholm,
Peter Glossop, Heather Begg, Roger Soyer,
Wandsworth School Boys' Choir, Royal Opera House
Chorus and Orchestra, Covent Garden
6709 002
Excerpts from complete recording
6500 161
4 7300 050

1969 November Berlioz. Requiem, Op. 5 (Grande
Messe des Morts)
with Ronald Dowd, Wandsworth School Boys' Choir,
LSO Chorus, LSO
6700 019

1970 July Tippett. THE MIDSUMMER MARRIAGE—complete
with Joan Carlyle, Alberto Remedios, Elizabeth Harwood, Stuart Burrows, Helen Watts, Raimund Herincx, Royal Opera House Chorus and Orchestra, Covent Garden   6703 027

1970 August Purcell. DIDO AND AENEAS—complete
with Josephine Veasey, Helen Donath, Delia Wallis, Elizabeth Bainbridge, Gillian Knight, Thomas Allen, John Shirley-Quirk, Frank Patterson, John Alldis Choir, Academy of St. Martin-in-the-Fields
                                    6500 131
                                    4 7300 073

1970 September Beethoven. Symphony No. 3 in E flat major, Op. 55, "Eroica"
BBC SO   6500 141
                                    4 7300 105

1970 September Beethoven. Piano Concerto No. 1 in C major, Op. 15
with Stephen Bishop (piano), BBC SO
                                    6500 179
                                    4 7300 116

1970 September Schumann. Piano Concerto in A minor, Op. 54
with Stephen Bishop (piano), BBC SO
                                    6500 166
                                    4 7300 113

1970 September "GERMAN OVERTURES"
Wagner. The Mastersingers of Nurnberg
Beethoven, Coriolan, Op. 62
Nicolai. The Merry Wives of Windsor
Mozart. The Magic Flute, K620
Mendelssohn. The Hebrides, Op. 26, "Fingals Cave"
Weber. Der Freischütz
BBC SO   6580 048
                                    4 7300 095

1971 January Grieg. Piano Concerto in A minor, Op. 16
with Stephen Bishop (piano), BBC SO
                                    6500 166
                                    4 7300 113

1971 January Mozart. Mass in C Minor, K. 427
Mass in C, K. 317, "Coronation" with Helen Donath, Gillian Knight, Ryland Davies, Stafford Dean, Clifford Grant, LSO Chorus, LSO.
                                    6500 234

1971 February Gerhard. Symphony No. 4
BBC SO   A. ZRG701

1971 February Mozart. Mass in C major, K259 "Great Mass" Helen Donath, Heather Harper, Ryland Davies, Stafford Dean, LSO Chorus, LSO
                                    6500 235

1971 April Gerhard. Violin Concerto with Yrfrah Neaman (violin), BBC SO
                          A. ZRG701

1971 April Mozart. LE NOZZE DI FIGARO—complete
with Jessye Norman, Mirella Freni, Maria Casula, Lillian Watson, Yvonne Minton, Robert Tear, Ingvar Wixell, Wladimiro Ganzarolli, Paul Hudson, Clifford Grant
BBC Chorus, BBC SO   6707 014
Excerpts from complete recording
                                    6500 434

1971 April Mozart. Vesperae solennes de confessore, K. 339
Exsultate, jubilate, K. 165
Kyrie in D Minor, K. 341
Ave verum corpus, K. 618
Kiri Te Kanawa, Elizabeth Bainbridge, Ryland Davies, Gwynne Howell, LSO Chorus, LSO.
                                    6500 271

1971 April Beethoven. Piano Concerto No. 3 in C Minor, Op. 37 Stephen Bishop, BBC SO
                                    6500 315
                                    4 7300 163

1971 July Wagner. Arias from Die Feen, Rienzi, Der Hiegende Holländer
                                    6500 294

1971 September Brahms. Violin Concerto in D, Op. 77
Arthur Grumiaux, New Philharmonia Orchestra.
                                    6500 299
                                    4 7300 202

1971 September Mozart. Symphony No. 38 in D, K. 504, "Prague"
Symphony No. 41 in C, K. 551 "Jupiter" BBC SO
                                    6500 313
                                    4 7300 200

1972 July Berlioz. Benvenuto Cellini—complete with Nicolai Gedda, Jules Bastin, Robert Massard, Roger Soyer, Derek Blackwell, Robert Lloyd, Raimund Herincx, Hugues Cuenod, Christiane Eda-Pierre, Jane Berbie, Janine Reiss, Chorus of the Royal Opera House, Covent Garden, BBC SO   6707 019